HEINEMANN HISTORY

CHINA IN THE 20TH CENTURY

HARRIET WARD

HEINEMANN
EDUCATIONAL

Heinemann Educational,
a division of Heinemann Educational Books Ltd,
Halley Court, Jordan Hill, Oxford OX2 8EJ

OXFORD LONDON EDINBURGH
MADRID ATHENS BOLOGNA PARIS
MELBOURNE SYDNEY AUCKLAND SINGAPORE TOKYO
IBADAN NAIROBI HARARE GABORONE
PORTSMOUTH NH (USA)

First published 1990

95 11 10 9 8 7 6 5 4

British Library Cataloguing in Publication Data

Ward, Harriet
    China in the 20th century − (Heinemann
    history).
    1. China, history
    I. Title
    951

ISBN 0−435−31038−0

Designed and produced by
The Pen and Ink Book Company Ltd, Huntingdon

Printed in Malta by Interprint Limited

Acknowledgements

The author and publisher would like to thank the following for permission to reproduce photographs on the pages indicated.

Anglo-Chinese Educational Institute: pp. 20 (right), 36, 46, (upper), 48, 51 and 52 (top); Camera Press Ltd: pp. 12 (top), 13, 46, and 52 (lower), Henri Cartier-Bresson: p. 29; Communist Party Picture Library: pp. 22 and 30 (lower); John Hillelson Agency Limited: pp. 7 (lower), 39, 40 and 58; Hulton-Deutsch Picture Company: pp. 15 and 24 (top); Magnum Photos: pp. 26, 34 (top), 42 and 58; Popperfoto: p. 34 (lower); Esther Samson: p. 32; Topham Picture Library: pp. 7 (top), 8, 20 (left), 25, 30 (top), 45 and 54; Roger Viollet: p. 10 (top); Xinhua News Agency: p. 16.

Cover photo by Anglo-Chinese Educational Institute.

The author and publisher would also like to thank the following for permission to reproduce copyright material:

The Geographical Journal for the graph which appears on page 54; Gollancz Ltd for the map by J. F. Horrabin taken from *The Post-War World: A Short Political History, 1918−1934* by J. Hampden Jackson which appears on page 19 (top); Jonathan Cape Ltd for the map which appears on page 19 (lower) and Macdonald & Co (Publishers) Ltd for the graph on page 43, taken from *Purnell's History of the Twentieth Century*.

We have been unable to contact the copyright holders of the photographs which appear on pages 8 and 10 (lower) and would be grateful for any information which would enable us to do so.

Details of Written Sources

In some sources the wording or sentence structure has been simplified to make sure that the source is accessible.

Jack Belden, *China Shakes the World*, Gollancz, 1950: 5.3A
Fox Butterfield, *China − Alive in the Bitter Sea*, Bantam, 1982: 4.4C and G
Esther Cheo Ying, *Black Country Girl in Red China*, Hutchinson, 1980: 4.2A, D and F, 4.7C

Brian Crozier, *The Man Who Lost China*, Angus & Robertson, 1976: 2.3B
John K Fairbank, *The United States and China*, Oxford University Press, 1959: 1.3G
Alun Falconer, *New China − Friend or Foe?*, The Naldrett Press Ltd, 1950: 5.5A
M. Fawdry, *Chinese Childhood*, Pollocks Toy Theatres Ltd, 1977: 1.3C
C. P. Fitzgerald, *Revolution in China*, Praeger, 1952: 3.7A
C. P. Fitzgerald, quoted in *History of the Twentieth Century*, Purnell, 1969: 3.6C, 3.7E
Peter Fleming, *One's Company − a Journey to China*, Jonathan Cape, 1934: 3.2A
Wolfgang Franke, *Century of Chinese Revolution 1859 − 1949*, Blackwell, 1980: 1.3H
J. Hampden Jackson, *The Post-War World: A Short Political History, 1918 − 1934*, Gollancz, 1935: 3.2B
Liang Heng and Judith Shapiro, *Return to China*, Chatto & Windus, 1987: 5.5E
Hugh Higgins, *From Warlords to Red Star*, Faber, 1968: 3.3C
Clare Hollingworth, *Mao and the Men against Him*, Cape, 1985: 4.11E
Immanuel C. Y. Hsü, *The Rise of Modern China*, Oxford University Press, 1970: 3.7G
Harold Isaacs, *The Tragedy of the Chinese Revolution*, Stanford University Press, 1962: 2.3D
Chiang Kaishek, *Soviet Russia in China − A Summing Up at Seventy*, Harrap, 1957: 2.3A, 3.7C
Fredric M. Kaplan and Julian M. Sobin, *Encyclopaedia of China Today*, Macmillan, 1982: 5.6D and E
Peter Lane, *China in the Twentieth Century*, Batsford, 1978: 2.3F
Robert Jay Lifton, *Thought Reform and the Psychology of Totalism*, Penguin, 1967: 4.5C, D and F
I. W. Mabbett, *Modern China: The Mirage of Modernity*, Croom Helm, 1985: 5.5B
Maria Macciocchi, *Daily Life in Revolutionary China*, Monthly Review Press, 1971: 4.10 B and C
Klaus Mehnert, *China Today*, Thames & Hudson, 1972: 4.10A
Edwin E. Moise, *Modern China*, Longman, 1986: 4.7D and G
Jan Myrdal, *Report from a Chinese Village*, Penguin, 1967: 4.4F
T. O. Newnham, *Three Chinese Communes*, Graphic Educational Publications Ltd, Auckland, 1967: 5.3B
Lynn Pan, *The New Chinese Revolution*, Hamish Hamilton, 1987: 5.2F, 5.3F
George Paloczi-Horvath, *Mao: Emperor of the Blue Ants*, Secker & Warburg, 1962: 4.11B
John Robottom, *Modern China*, Longman, 1967: 1.3F
Harrison Salisbury, *The Long March: The Untold Story*, Macmillan, 1985: 3.4C
Stuart Schram, *Mao Zedong*, Penguin, 1966: 4.7F
F. Schurmann and O. Schell, *China Readings 1: Imperial China*, Penguin, 1967: 1.2A and B
F. Schurmann and O. Schell, *China Readings 3: Communist China*, Penguin, 1967: 4.8A
Ruth Sidel, *Women and Child Care in China − A Firsthand Report*, Sheldon Press, 1972: 4.4B
Edgar Snow, *Red Star over China*, Gollancz, 1937: 3.4A, 4.11C
Jonathan Spence, *The Gate of Heavenly Peace*, Penguin, 1982: 1.3A and B, 2.1A
Barbara W. Tuchman, *Stilwell and the American Experience in China, 1911–45*, Bantam, 1972: 2.3E
Marina Warner, *The Dragon Empress*, Weidenfeld & Nicolson, 1972: 1.3E
Dick Wilson, *Mao, the People's Emperor*, Hutchinson, 1979: 4.11A
Alan Winnington, *Breakfast with Mao*, Lawrence & Wishart, 1986: 4.5A and B, 4.7B
D. Zagonia, 'Russia and China − Two Roads to Communism', in *Survey: a Journal of Soviet and East European Studies*, October 1961: 4.8D

CONTENTS

1.1 THE CHALLENGE OF THE WEST

For hundreds of years the Chinese believed their **Celestial Empire** was the centre of the universe. Their **Emperor** was known as the 'Son of Heaven, Ruler of the World', and they considered themselves superior to all other peoples – **barbarians** and **foreign devils** as the Chinese called them. By 1800 the Empire included Manchuria, Mongolia, Xinjiang, Tibet and the island of Formosa (now called Taiwan). Beyond these lands, an outer ring of **tributary states** made an annual payment (tribute) to the Chinese Emperor as their overlord.

Contact with European traders

The rulers of China believed they needed nothing from the outside world. In 1793 the Emperor explained to a representative of the British King George III: 'As your Ambassador can see for himself, we possess all things. I set no value on objects strange or ingenious, and have no use for your country's manufactures.'

By resisting Britain's attempts to expand trade with China, the imperial government kept China isolated until well into the nineteenth century. But eventually China had to yield. Frustrated in their efforts to sell manufactured goods to China, British traders found something else to exchange for the silks, tea and luxury goods that Europeans wanted. By the 1820s the notorious, illegal **opium trade** was developing fast.

The opium was grown in British India and Bengal, shipped to the coast of China and then smuggled ashore with the help of corrupt Chinese agents. The Chinese government's attempts to stop the harmful traffic led to the **Opium Wars** of **1839–42** and **1856–60** between Britain and China, in which the Chinese were no match for the superior British armoury. In 1860 an Anglo-French force even reached Beijing (Peking) and burned down the Emperor's summer palace.

The **Treaty of Nanjing of 1842** was the first of a series of **unequal treaties** (as the Chinese called them, because China was an unwilling and unequal partner) which brought the proud Chinese empire to its knees by the end of the century. Britain gained **Hong Kong** as a colony. China was forced to open up a string of **treaty ports** along the coast and up the Yangzi River, to allow foreign nations to trade in China. These coastal cities were also a gateway into China for the many groups of **Christian missionaries** who were just as eager to save Chinese souls as the traders were to sell their products.

Within the treaty ports were **concession areas** where the Beijing government was forced to allow foreigners to live and work without interference. The exclusion of Chinese law and the Chinese police from these areas was very irritating to the Chinese authorities. Not only could foreigners escape Chinese law, but Chinese plotters against the government sometimes took refuge in the concession areas.

The power of the Chinese Empire was further reduced by the loss of land in the north-east to Russia, while the tributary states were colonized by other empire-builders (see map). In the 1880s **Burma** came under British rule, and **Indo-China** fell to France.

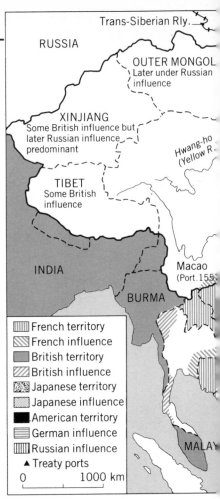

French territory
French influence
British territory
British influence
Japanese territory
Japanese influence
American territory
German influence
Russian influence
▲ Treaty ports
0   1000 km

Foreign encroachment on China, 1911. The treaty ports were open to European traders from the dates indicated.

SOURCE A

Contemporary cartoon of British mission to China, 1793.

Japan had already annexed the **Ryukyu Islands** and was now showing interest in **Korea**. Japan's advances were especially dangerous for China.

Threat from Japan
In the 1860s under a far-sighted Emperor who saw the way the world was going, **Japan** began a programme of rapid **modernization**. By the 1890s its expanding industry demanded resources and markets, and the nearby mainland of China was a tempting area for exploitation.

In 1894 Japan and China came to blows over Korea. Japan easily won the fighting. By the **Treaty of Shimonoseki of 1895** Japan gained **Taiwan** and a strong influence in **Korea** (which became a Japanese colony in 1910). Next Japan challenged Russia for control of **Manchuria**, where China had already granted Russia the right to build a railway, and a lease on **Port Arthur**. After a disastrous defeat in the **Russo-Japanese War** of 1904–5, Russia gave up these possessions to Japan.

Suppression of the Boxer Rebellion
By 1898 Britain, Germany and France had gained exclusive trading rights in **spheres of influence** around the treaty ports. The United States was anxious not to be left out of these arrangements. It put pressure on China to accept an '**open door**' policy of free trading in the Chinese market for all nations on equal terms. In fact foreign influence in China was not confined to any 'sphere' but spread through all aspects of economic life. Foreigners ran the Post Office, supervised the Customs, built and staffed the railways, and set up banks, insurance and shipping companies. Foreign gunboats patrolled China's inland waterways. Patriotic Chinese deeply resented the way their country had been taken over, and many blamed their own government for allowing it to happen.

In 1900 came the badly organized and unsuccessful **Boxer Rebellion** against the 'foreign devils'. Unofficially encouraged by the Chinese government, members of the secret **League of Harmonious Fists** (the **Boxers**) besieged the foreign embassies in Beijing, killing the German ambassador and other foreign personnel. The German Kaiser organized an eight-nation relief force to avenge the victims. In the face of the wrathful foreigners the imperial government fled Beijing – only to return shamefacedly to submit to the **International Protocol of 1901**. This protocol forced China to pay huge sums of compensation to the offended powers and to accept the stationing of their troops in Beijing and eleven other cities 'to keep order'. The humiliation of the Celestial Empire was complete.

1.2 THE DECAY OF A PROUD EMPIRE

The Chinese way of life and system of government were based on the teachings of the ancient philosopher **Confucius**. Confucius taught that the Emperor held his throne on God's authority; and even a foreign ruler should be respected and obeyed so long as he or she governed well and wisely. But if a ruler ceased to govern well he or she lost Heaven's permission to rule and could be overthrown. This had last happened in 1644, when conquerors from Manchuria (the north-east corner of present-day China) overthrew the weakened Ming Dynasty and placed the **Manchu Dynasty** in power.

The 5 million ruling Manchus came to have many privileges which were resented by their 400 million Chinese subjects. For example, entry to **government service** was meant to be based on merit rather than wealth or birth. The **mandarins** (officials) had to pass a competitive examination to each level of administration, and in theory these were open to any citizen. But over the years these examinations had become a dry and pointless exercise on classical texts, which no peasant's son had the time or the education to study for. The civil service grew inefficient and corrupt (see Source A).

The Taiping Rebellion

The people's dissatisfaction with their rulers frequently boiled over. From 1851 to 1864 the **Taiping Rebellion** kept the Manchu armies very busy. It was finally put down with the help of **General Gordon**, lent to the Emperor by the British government because the rebels' activities were disturbing British trade. The Taipings, led by a converted Christian, held some beliefs similar to the ideas of Communism. They proposed a share-out of land and wealth, and a society in which women had equal rights with men. The rebellion ravaged two-thirds of the Empire, at a cost of over 20 milllion lives.

From the numbers who supported the Taipings, and the millions who would follow the Communists eighty years later, you can guess that these revolutionaries had hit upon some of China's real problems. Ninety per cent of the Chinese were **peasants** scraping a bare living from the soil. What they grew in summer was eaten in the winter – *if* the weather was kind and *if* the landlord or the tax-collector didn't get it first. Many peasants paid very high rents to absentee landlords, but even those who owned their land often had too little to support a family. A steady rise in population, from 100 million in 1750 to 400 million by 1835, coupled with the practice of dividing farms among all the sons from one generation to the next, had reduced the average holding to half an acre – scarcely more than a large garden.

The subjection of women

One 'asset' the peasant might be forced to sell in hard times was his wife or daughter. In Old China, as in many other peasant societies, a **woman** was the property first of her father, then of her husband. A daughter was often an unwelcome arrival in a poor family, for as a child she would hardly earn her keep, and on

SOURCE C

The Empress Dowager Cixi in 1903.

SOURCE D

◀ *Chinese street scene: a public letter writer and a barber at work.*

marriage she joined her husband's family. A son, on the other hand, would bring his wife's labour to his father's household. For this reason, girl babies were sometimes drowned or left to die in the fields.

At every level of society above the poorest peasants and coolies (labourers) a further cruel indignity placed on a girl was the practice of **foot-binding**. This produced the deformed 'lily feet' which were considered a mark of beauty and of social status. From the age of 5 or 6, bandages were bound tightly round a girl's feet, crushing the four smaller toes under the sole until the bones gradually broke and reset to form a pointed stump of a foot scarcely three inches long. For years a growing girl suffered constant pain, and as an adult she could only totter along awkwardly when she walked unaided. Yet only a few parents dared to defy social custom to spare their daughters this torture (see pages 8–9).

Reform and revolution

Increasing contacts with the outside world made middle-class Chinese aware and ashamed of their nation's backwardness. Some believed that change was possible without destroying the existing system, but the **Empress Dowager Cixi**, who held power in China after 1861, blocked every move for change and blindly disregarded her country's needs.

Other reformers had long given up hope of any progress until the corrupt and hateful Manchu government was overthrown. With the example of Japan before their eyes, they wanted to modernize China along Western lines. Above all they were **nationalists**, wanting a strong, independent government which would expel the foreign exploiters and restore China's national pride. Their leader was **Dr Sun Yatsen**, a graduate of Hong Kong medical school, who had given up doctoring for work he considered more important – the salvation of China.

Sun Yatsen had travelled widely in the West and hoped that China would eventually become a liberal democracy like Britain or the United States. But in the Manchu Empire his only choice was to be a revolutionary. After 1895 he divided his time between organizing revolutions in China – there were ten attempts before the one that succeeded – and touring the world to raise funds. In 1908 both the Emperor and the Empress Dowager died, leaving no strong personality to cling on to power. Sun Yatsen was in the USA when the **Double Tenth Rebellion** of 10 October 1911 finally toppled the Manchu government. In December he returned home to become the provisional President of the new-born **Republic of China**.

1.3 QIU JIN – WOMAN REVOLUTIONARY

EMPATHY

Millions of illiterate peasant women in nineteenth-century China had no way of improving their situation or of escaping from it. They would have to wait many years for a chance to tell their story, and for a measure of liberation. But by the turn of the century a handful of middle-class women were beginning to break the bonds of convention and to ask for basic human rights. One of these was **Qiu Jin**, whose views seem far ahead of her time (Source A).

Qiu Jin felt imprisoned in an arranged marriage to a husband she hated. In 1904, at the age of 26, she abandoned him and her son and daughter and took ship for Japan. There she joined other young Chinese exiles in a ferment of revolutionary talk and activity. She became a member of Sun Yatsen's Revolutionary Alliance, formed in Japan in 1905 to co-ordinate several anti-Manchu organizations.

Qiu Jin was homesick and always short of money. In 1905 her brother wrote on behalf of her family to urge her to return to her husband, but Qiu Jin indignantly refused (Source B). In 1906 she did return to China, but not to her husband. She was now able to support herself as a writer and a teacher. Together with a male cousin she became involved in one of the many unsuccessful plots to overthrow the Manchu government. They were rather careless conspirators and soon attracted the attention of the authorities. In July 1907 they were both caught and executed. Qiu Jin was 29 when she died, one of the first women martyrs of the Chinese Revolution.

SOURCE B

'That person's behaviour is worse than an animal's. Now that he has seized my remaining jewellery, how can we even think of him as being human? My treatment in that household was worse than a slave's; the poison of hatred has eaten deeply into me. Send my sister to try to get my money back – if he won't give it up, then break off all relations. I have thought this through thoroughly: rather than be treated as a slave, why should I not stand up for myself? Henceforth I am going to try to support myself through my own efforts; why should I be somebody's wife? There has been no letter from him for over a year, he has shown no respect to his seniors in my family, and I have also heard that he has taken a new wife.'

Qiu Jin's reply to her brother's advice to return to her husband in 1905.

SOURCE A

'Women must get educated and strive for their own independence; they can't just go on asking men for everything. The young intellectuals are all chanting, "Revolution! Revolution!" But I say the revolution will have to start in our homes, by achieving equal rights for women.'

Letter from Qiu Jin to a woman friend, 1906.

SOURCE C

'When a son is born, he sleeps in a bed, plays with pearls and is dressed in fine robes: he is a prince who has everyone at his beck and call. But when a girl is born, she is put on the ground with only a thin coverlet, her only toy a bit of broken tile. She is good for nothing, except to prepare food and wine and not to cause her parents any trouble.'

Comment by a nineteenth-century Chinese poet.

◄ *Qiu Jin.*

SOURCE D

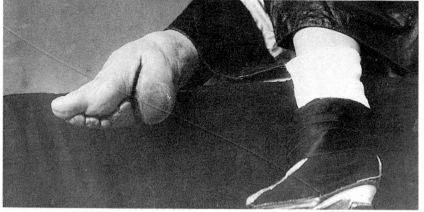

A Chinese woman's feet deformed by lifelong binding.

SOURCE H

'The equality of men and women practised by the Taipings was a revolutionary act of great importance. Women, like men, now could take the state examinations and could hold civil or military offices; there were special female units in the Taiping army. Foot-binding was strictly forbidden, as was prostitution; white slavery and rape were punished by death. Marriage was compulsory; women and girls who did not have the protection of male family members were particularly taken care of.'

Wolfgang Franke, 'Century of Chinese Revolution, 1859–1949', 1980.

SOURCE E

'In her tiny embroidered shoes, with beribboned pantaloons falling prettily over the swollen and deformed ankles, or in elegant spats, the Chinese girl minced along daintily on the arm of one of her sons or one of her servants. This was the famous 'lily walk', for the movement of her figure as she tottered on her cramped and crippled feet was celebrated in thousands of years of prose and verse, even though, when the bandages were renewed, the stench of compressed flesh was appalling.'

Marina Warner, 'The Dragon Empress', 1972.

SOURCE G

'A girl's marriage was, of course, arranged and not for love. The trembling bride bacame at once a daughter-in-law under the tyranny of her husband's mother. In a well-to-do family she might see secondary wives (concubines) brought into the household, particularly if she did not bear a male heir. A woman had no economic independence. Her work was devoted to household tasks and brought her no income. The crippling practice by which a young girl's feet were tightly wrapped to prevent normal development seems to have begun about the tenth century AD. The 'lily feet' which it produced through the suffering of hundreds of millions of young girls acquired great artistic and sexual value. In practice bound feet kept womankind from venturing far abroad.'

SOURCE F

'Sun Yatsen pleaded with his mother to unbind his sister's feet and relieve her pain. But, like all devoted Chinese mothers, she refused and the binding was only taken off when his sister's deformity had become permanent.'

John Robottom, 'Modern China', 1986.

John K. Fairbank, 'The United States and China', 1959.

EXERCISE

1 a Why do you think Sun Yatsen's mother insisted that her daughter had her feet bound (Source F)? Explain your answer.
  b Why do you think Sun Yatsen wanted her not to? Explain your answer.

2 Do you think Qiu Jin would have supported the ideas of the Taipings (Source H)? Give reasons for your answer.

3 Chinese peasant women had no chance to act in the way Qiu Jin did. How do you think they would have felt about her actions?

4 Do you think the treatment of women in China at this time proves that Chinese men were deliberately cruel? Give reasons for your answer.

2.1 WARLORDS AND REFORMERS, 1911–21

Yuan Shikai and the warlords

After the **Double Tenth Rebellion** of 1911 (see pages 6–7), the southern provinces of China supported **Sun Yatsen**. But the Manchu family was still in Beijing, protected by the imperial army. The army's cunning commander-in-chief, **Yuan Shikai**, now offered to bring the army over to support the Republic – if he could be its President. Sun Yatsen unwisely agreed. Yuan then found it 'inconvenient' to move to the Republic's intended new capital at Nanjing and continued to run the government from the imperial capital of Beijing. All this was part of Yuan's plan to make himself the new Emperor. He organized 'popular demand' for his enthronement in 1916, but at the last moment jealous army commanders opposed it. Yuan dropped his plans and a few months later he died – of 'eating bitterness', the Chinese said.

With Yuan Shikai's death in 1916 China moved from political chaos to worse political chaos. This was the period of **warlord rule**. The warlords, each with his private army, were a varied group. Some were provincial governors appointed by Yuan; others were little more than bandits whose only aim was to make a personal fortune and then retire to a foreign concession where it could be stashed away in a foreign bank. For the next twelve years the warlords fought each other, singly or in groups, for the control of territory and revenue. The greatest prize – which sometimes changed hands more than once in a year – was to control the official government at Beijing, with its considerable income from customs duties and taxes.

Conditions for China's millions of peasants worsened during these years. Banditry and lawlessness increased. Landlords fled to the towns, leaving their rents to be collected by agents who called in local military men to help – for a cut, of course. Local government officials also squeezed the villages. In Sichuan province in 1923, taxes had been collected in advance up to 1968!

Sun Yatsen's political revolution, now led by his **Nationalist Party**, the **Guomindang (GMD)**, slowed to a stop in the warlord era. But other aspects of the Chinese Revolution were flourishing even at this chaotic time.

SOURCE B

A street execution in a warlord's capital.

SOURCE C

SOURCE A

'The patriotic movement had a deeper meaning than mere patriotism. The taste of colonialism in its full bitterness had never come home to the Chinese until then, even though we already had the experience of decades of foreign exploitation behind us. The sharp pain of imperialistic oppression then reached our bones, and it awakened us from the nightmares of impractical democratic reforms. The issue of the former German possessions in Shandong, which started the uproar of the student movement, could not be separated from the larger problem.'

Qu Qiubai, a 20-year-old student at the time, remembers the May Fourth protest. He later became a leader of the Chinese Communist Party.

Police break up a student demonstration, Beijing, May 1919. ▼

The reformers of 'Young China'

The fall of the Manchu government spurred on the young intellectuals of China. They were already busy overturning what they called the '**olds**' of Confucian thought and behaviour which had so restricted previous generations. One of these 'olds' was the tradition that all serious literature had to be written in classical Chinese, a 'dead' language so difficult that only a handful of scholars ever learned it. Professors at Beijing University now led the move to popularize a much simpler form of the language, close to ordinary speech. This reform spread the **new ideas** and literature to a growing middle class, by now numbering 10 or 12 million in China's main cities, and later made possible the **mass education** essential to a modern society.

The young intellectuals eagerly welcomed Western ideas. They wanted the Chinese to study 'Mr Science' and 'Mr Democracy' rather than Confucius. They debated excitedly whether change should come gradually, 'by inches and drops', or more quickly, through revolution. Among those who argued that China could not wait for 'inches and drops' of reform was a young assistant librarian at Beijing University, **Mao Zedong**.

The May Fourth Movement

This debate was influenced by events outside China. In 1919 the victorious Allies of the **First World War** met at **Versailles** in France to draw up a peace settlement. One of their declared aims was to guarantee all nations the right to choose their own government. The young Republic of China therefore hoped the great powers would respect its wish to be free of foreign control, and that defeated Germany's possessions in **Shandong** province would be returned to China. The Chinese did not know that Britain and France had secretly promised Japan that it could take over German possessions in China after the war.

There was outrage in China when this shady deal was revealed at the Versailles Conference. On **4 May 1919** there was a near-riot by 5,000 students in Beijing. Demonstrations in other cities followed, then several months of strikes and boycotts of Japanese goods. These events gave a political focus – and the name **May Fourth Movement** – to the cultural and political awakening of 'Young China' (see Source A).

Birth of the Chinese Communist Party

Disillusioned with what they saw as the hypocrisy of the Western democracies, most of the leaders of the May Fourth Movement now saw more hope for China in **Communism**. After the **Bolshevik Revolution** in **Russia** in 1917, the Communists had not only overthrown the old order along with their Tsar but by 1921 had also repulsed military attacks by the Western powers and Japan. They set up a new state, the **Union of Soviet Socialist Republics** (USSR or Soviet Union for short), and established an organization, the **Comintern**, to spread Communism to other countries. In 1921 the Comintern helped to found the **Chinese Communist Party (CCP)** in Shanghai.

2.2 NATIONALIST CHINA, 1921–37

The Guomindang gathers support

After Yuan Shikai's treachery (see pages 10–11), Sun Yatsen formed a rival government in the southern city of **Guangzhou** (Canton), but for many years it was very insecure. In 1921 he announced his political programme, the **Three People's Principles** which became the official policy of the Guomindang (GMD) Party. The three principles were:

- **Nationalism**   The Chinese people were like 'a sheet of loose sand', said Sun. They must be united under a central government strong enough to expel foreign influence and restore China's national independence.
- **Democracy**   Sun's long-term aim was a democratic system on the Western model, but there would have to be a transition period to educate the people for self-government, during which the GMD would rule as a dictatorship.
- **People's livelihood**   Sun wanted economic development along socialist lines – that is, to provide a fair distribution of wealth. The most urgent reform was to give 'the land to the tiller' (the person who worked it).

Although he was not a Communist, Sun envied the Communists' success in Russia. When the Soviet Union offered help to achieve this programme, he gladly accepted. In 1923 a three-way alliance of the GMD, the Comintern and the Chinese Communist Party (CCP) was formed. Under this **United Front** the Soviet government sent advisers, money and arms to the GMD, and CCP members were welcomed into its ranks.

During the United Front period the GMD gained contacts with workers and peasants through its Communist members. It also developed an efficient National Revolutionary Army headed by **Chiang Kaishek**, who was trained in the Soviet Union. By July 1926 the GMD was ready to launch its **Northern Expedition** against the warlords. The southern provinces were soon won over (see map). In January 1927 the government moved to the city of **Wuhan**, while Chiang's army prepared to capture Nanjing and Shanghai. Then came a serious political crisis.

Sun Yatsen had died suddenly in 1925, leaving his party split between the GMD **Left**, in control of the Wuhan government, and the **Right**, led by Chiang Kaishek, commander of the army. The Left wanted to continue the alliance with the CCP; but Chiang was deeply suspicious of Communist influence. In April 1927 Chiang ordered the **Shanghai massacre** of Communist labour leaders, followed by similar purges in other cities, and then declared a rival government at Nanjing. By July the Left had given way. The Communists were expelled from the GMD, the Soviet advisers were sent home, and the GMD was reunited – on Chiang's terms and under his leadership (see pages 14–5).

Chiang now quickly consolidated his power. By 1928 his forces had taken Beijing, and the foreign nations agreed to deal with the new Nationalist government at **Nanjing**. It would rule China for the next twenty-one years.

Sun Yatsen, seated, with his successor Chiang Kaishek in 1923.

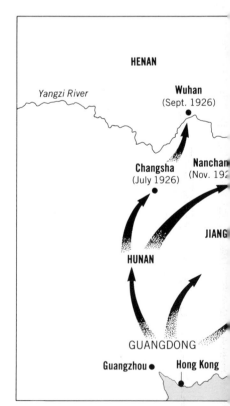

HENAN

Yangzi River

Wuhan
(Sept. 1926)

Changsha
(July 1926)

Nanchan
(Nov. 192

JIANG

HUNAN

GUANGDONG

Guangzhou ●   Hong Kong

SOURCE **B**

Michael Borodin, Soviet adviser to the GMD, with one of his Chinese staff in Guangzhou.

Nanjing
(March 1927)

Shanghai

Hangzhou
(Feb. 1927)

AN

Limited progress, 1928–37

The Guomindang had only ten years to prove itself worthy to rule China before the nation was plunged into a devastating war with Japan. But it failed to do so. Chiang Kaishek's Nationalist government had the following serious weaknesses:

- **Limited control of the country**   The warlords were never completely conquered; they just submitted to Chiang as a 'super-warlord'. The outer fringes of the old Empire remained beyond his control, and even in the heartland of China local strongmen were liable to rebel if his attention was distracted. Also undermining his authority, as Chiang well knew, were the '**Red base areas**' set up by the Communist survivors of the 1927 purge (see pages 18–9). Chiang spent much effort on his military campaigns against them, to the neglect of other national problems.

- **A narrow political base**   Without its left-wing members and their contacts with workers and peasants, the GMD became more and more a conservative, middle-class and city-based party. Many of its supporters were landowners who opposed reforms which might benefit the peasants.

- **Internal corruption**   The reforming spririt of the GMD seemed to die with Sun Yatsen. Its members were loyal to powerful family groups rather than to the organization as a whole or to the Chinese nation. Corrupt officials of warlord governments were allowed into the service of the Republic, where they continued to line their own pockets. Chiang himself became more and more dictatorial, copying some features of Nazi rule in Germany which he admired.

- **No change for peasants**   Progress under the Nationalist government mainly helped its own supporters. By 1937 the cities were benefiting from improved transport, communications and education. Foreign interference in commercial life was reduced. But in China's vast countryside, little had changed. In the 1930s the size of landholdings actually increased, which meant that even more peasants had none or too little. Thousands continued to die in floods and famine, scarcely noticed by the Nanjing government.

What had become of Sun Yatsen's Three People's Principles? Chiang's government did not cement the 'loose sand', or introduce democracy, or give land to the tiller. But in the end it was his neglect of the principle of **nationalism** that lost Chiang Kaishek the support of the Chinese people. That was a trump card (only one of them) of his rival, **Mao Zedong**.

◀ *The GMD's Northern Expedition, 1926–7.
Dates in brackets show the date of capture.*

2.3 THE SHANGHAI MASSACRE OF 1927

EVIDENCE

The coalition formed in 1923 between the **Guomindang** and the **Chinese Communist Party** was always an uneasy partnership. While Sun Yatsen lived he kept it together, but when he died in 1925 his party fell into opposing factions. The **Left** under **Wang Jingwei** wanted to continue the alliance with the CCP and the Comintern advisers, while the **Right** led by **Chiang Kaishek**, commander of the army, suspected a Communist plot to take over the GMD.

The issue came to a head during the **Northern Expedition of 1926–7** against the warlords. By January 1927 the government, in the hands of the GMD Left, had moved north from Guangzhou to **Wuhan**. Nanjing was taken in March, and Chiang Kaishek then proposed to strike east to **Shanghai**, the main stronghold of foreign interests in China. In anticipation of his arrival, Communist-led trade unions mobilized 100,000 workers to seize control of the city from the local warlord; their armed pickets now stood ready to hand it over to the triumphant Nationalist army. In the concession areas were several thousand foreign residents, much alarmed by recent violence in Nanjing in which six foreigners had been killed.

The foreigners need not have worried. Instead of joining hands with his Communist allies, Chiang destroyed them in the **Shanghai massacre** of 12 April 1927, a slaughter repeated in other cities. Chiang set up a rival government at **Nanjing** and within a few months the Left had accepted Chiang's view of the Communists as dangerous infiltrators and gave its allegiance to his government. Chiang was now the undisputed leader of the Guomindang and so he remained until his death in exile in 1975.

Historians rightly see the Shanghai massacre as a turning-point in China's history. Under Chiang the GMD turned sharp right to link up with the business people and financiers who had little interest in social reform. It sent the Communist survivors of the purges into the countryside of China, where their own successful revolution would be forged in the coming years. Yet the precise details of this crucial event of 1927 have never been established. Exactly how did Chiang 'arrange' the disarming and killing of the Shanghai Communists? Did he enlist the sinister Green and Red secret societies – and even the hated foreigners – to carry out his work?

SOURCE A

'On 12 April, to prevent Communist uprisings, our Revolutionary Forces, in co-operation with local labour unions and chambers of commerce, disarmed Red labour pickets and kept Communist saboteurs under surveillance. Only then was the situation in Shanghai brought under control.'

Chiang Kaishek's own account of the events in Shanghai.

SOURCE B

'What happened in Shanghai is obscure and probably always will be. One account says the Communists hired local ruffians and "bandit-soldiers of the local warlord" and put them in the uniforms of the Labour Union Corps. On 12 April, led by the Communists and accompanied by their wives and children (Tong goes on), the rowdies surrounded and attacked the headquarters of the 26th Army Corps.

'But there is an alternative version – that it was the Guomindang who had put the local gangsters into labour uniforms. At a given signal, the false labour leaders attacked the working-class organizations throughout the city and shot all who resisted and many who did not. A more extreme version of the same story alleges that Chiang Kaishek had reached a prior arrangement with the secret society leader, Tu Yueh-sheng, before entering Shanghai. Green Society gangsters, together with the fascist Blue Shirts, were said to have massacred "thousands" of labour leaders and militant workers. Thousands? Even the CCP is less sweeping in its claims. The official Communist figures are 300 killed and 5,000 "missing".'

Brian Crozier, 'The Man Who Lost China', 1976.

SOURCE C

Bodies of Communists in the streets of Shanghai, April 1927.

SOURCE D

'The attack came as no surprise to anyone except the workers, for as the local British newspaper revealed: "All the authorities concerned, Chinese and foreign, after midnight were made secretly aware of the events which were to take place in the morning."

'Members of Shanghai's underworld gangs "had feverishly worked through the night organizing secret parties to appear at dawn as though from nowhere". More bluntly, another reporter said:
"Arrangements were made with the Green and Red societies, so that one morning they fell upon and shot down the Communists."'

Harold Isaacs, 'The Tragedy of the Chinese Revolution', 1962.

SOURCE E

'Chiang Kaishek made a wide sweep. On the night of 11–12 April, assisted by agents of the Green Society and police of the French Concession, he carried out a bloody purge of the left, disarming and hunting down all who could be found and killing more than 300.'

Barbara W. Tuchman, 'Stilwell and the American Experience in China, 1911–45', 1972.

SOURCE F

'Chiang called on his friends among the secret societies in Shanghai and, with the aid of his more loyal troops, he attacked the Communists who, along with the trade unionists, were arrested and shot; Russian advisers were expelled, the Communist organizations and offices smashed. Over 5,000 people died in Shanghai alone; thousands of others suffered in other towns and cities.'

Peter Lane, 'China in the Twentieth Century', 1978.

EXERCISE

1 Why do you think Chiang Kaishek did not mention the killings?

2 What does Source B prove? Give reasons for your answer.

3 The author of Source B gives three explanations for the killings:
  • the Communists hired local bandits
  • the Guomindang hired local gangsters
  • Chiang did a deal with Tu Yueh-sheng, leader of the Green Society, an organization of Shanghai gangsters.
Which of these explanations do you think the author of Source B believes? Give reasons for your answer.

4 Is Source D a primary or a secondary source? Explain your answer.

5 a Does Source C help you to decide which of the explanations in Source B to believe? Explain your answer.
  b Does Source D help you to decide which of the explanations in Source B to believe? Explain your answer.
  c Does Source E help you to decide which of the explanations in Source B to believe? Explain your answer.

6 Do you think that Source F is a reasonable judgement about the Shanghai Massacre to put in a school textbook? Give reasons for your answer.

7 What evidence other than the sources here would a historian need to be sure what happened in Shanghai? Explain your answer.

3.1 WORKING WITH THE PEASANTS, 1927–34

When **Mao Zedong** wrote Source A in 1927 his optimism was hardly justified. After the **Shanghai massacre** in April (see pages 14–5) the Chinese Communist Party was further weakened when its attempts to seize several cities were all decisively defeated. So was Mao's own effort to create a 'mighty storm' of peasants in the **Autumn Harvest Uprising** in September. Mao and many other survivors fled to the hills of south-eastern China, while most of the CCP leaders went 'underground' in Shanghai.

The CCP's Soviet connection

Mao was already beginning to realize that in a peasant country a successful revolution must be based on the peasants. This idea went directly against the understanding of Marxism that other CCP leaders, under the direction of the **Comintern**, were trying to bring about in China. They believed in Marx's prediction that the Communist revolution would be led by the **proletariat** (factory workers) in the cities. Both Marx and his Russian disciple **Lenin** thought that peasants were too backward, too selfish and too isolated – each family tied to its plot of land – to be organized into an effective revolutionary force.

So the Comintern always advised the CCP that its task was to rouse the working class in the cities and not waste time in a 'side current' working with the peasants. This instruction led to the unsuccessful city revolts of 1927, and Mao was reprimanded for his attempted peasant rising.

After Lenin's death in 1924 the new Soviet leader **Stalin** concentrated on strengthening the Soviet Union rather than spreading Communism to other countries. In China, Soviet national interests were always more important to him than the fate of the CCP. But for many years no Chinese Communist leader dared to question the 'expert' advice from Moscow transmitted through the Comintern.

The Jiangxi soviet

By the middle of 1928 the Communist survivors of disasters in the cities had set up several '**Red bases**' in the countryside, most importantly the **Jiangxi soviet** in Jiangxi province. Here, Mao and other leaders began to develop a winning formula for their Communist revolution: political and economic work with the peasants, and a **Red Army** skilled in mobile warfare.

In the Communist-controlled areas the CCP did not at first launch a fierce assault on the rural ruling classes. Surplus land was taken from those who had it and redistributed more or less equally to everyone. Landlords and rich peasants were usually allowed a fair share and encouraged to take part in the **peasants' associations** set up to run village affairs. With this soft-footed approach the Jiangxi soviet steadily expanded to include about 3 million people, with its own schools, hospitals and workshops.

SOURCE A

'In a very short time, in China's central, southern and northern provinces, several hundred million peasants will rise like a mighty storm, like a hurricane, a force so swift and violent that no power, however great, will be able to hold it back.'

Mao Zedong, 'Report on an Investigation of the Peasant Movement in Hunan', February 1927.

SOURCE B

SOURCE C

'The enemy advances, we retreat; the enemy camps, we harass; the enemy tires, we attack; the enemy retreats, we pursue.'

The 'eight-character slogan' that Red Army officers knew by heart.

Before moving to Jiangxi early in 1929 Mao had spent a difficult period in the bandit country of the **Jinggangshan mountains**, where he formed a long-lasting partnership with **Zhu De**. Zhu became commander-in-chief of the Red Army and Mao its political adviser.

The early recruits were a raggle-taggle crew of bandits and Guomindang prisoners who might return to banditry or the GMD after a defeat (and there were many at that time). But the peasants recruited in Jiangxi had seen some benefits of Communism, and were keen to spread the word. They won many converts among the wretchedly poor villagers who were used to being robbed and raped by warlord armies.

Between 1930 and 1934 Chiang Kaishek sent five major **'bandit-extermination campaigns'** against the soviets (see pages 18–21). The strategy developed by Zhu and Mao was to 'melt away' ahead of an advancing Nationalist column and thus draw it deep into Communist territory, where small groups of the enemy could be cut off from the main force and wiped out. Mobility and flexibility were the essence of this hit-and-run warfare. 'Fight when you can win; move away when you cannot win,' wrote Mao in an essay on military strategy. Source C is his well-known summary of Red Army tactics.

Other leaders, other policies

Mao was an important figure in the Jiangxi soviet, but the leadership of the CCP was still in the hands of Moscow-directed officials in Shanghai. In 1930 they ordered a return to the policy of attacking cities, but it was just as unsuccessful and costly in lives as the same policy had been in 1927. Once again the CCP turned to its 'side current' work in Jiangxi, which now came under the direction of a group known as the **twenty-eight Bolsheviks**. These were a group of young Chinese just returned from studying in Moscow, who were out of touch with what had been going on in the rural soviets of China.

The new leaders had learned their Marxism in the classroom and insisted on textbook policies. **Class warfare** was hotted up. A new Land Law of 1931 decreed that landlords and rich peasants must be entirely dispossessed and their wealth shared out among the poorest peasants. Only thus, argued these Moscow-style Marxists, would the age-old power of the rural élite be broken. They also disliked Zhu and Mao's military strategy which allowed invading troops into Communist territory; instead, they wanted the Red Army to defend the borders of the soviet and its civilian population. But for the time being the Red Army commanders defied the 'armchair strategists' and continued their successful mobile warfare.

◀ *A meeting of the first All-China Congress of Soviets, held in Ruijin, Jiangxi province, in November 1931. Mao Zedong is in the centre, with Zhu De on his left.*

3.2 # THE 'RED BANDITS' IN 1934

EVIDENCE

To the outside world China seemed relatively peaceful in the early 1930s. The Nationalist government established at Nanjing in 1928 was now internationally recognized as the ruler of all China. Outsiders heard little about Communism in the countryside. Chiang Kaishek always minimized the importance of the 'Red bandits', and the Communists themselves had no regular communication with the outside world. But there was great curiosity about the extent of Communist strength and whether it would become a real threat to Chiang Kaishek's government.

The sources in this unit were written and published between 1933 and 1935. Source A is by an Englishman who spent five months travelling in China during 1933; his route is indicated in Source D, taken from his book. Source B and its accompanying map, Source C, are from a work of **contemporary history** — that is, history written very soon after the events it describes.

Note that these sources use the form of English spelling of Chinese names in use when they were written, so that the province we know as Jiangxi appears here as Kiangsi. You will have no difficulty identifying other names and places mentioned.

SOURCE A

'The Red Armies are commanded by Chu Teh, a general of experience and resource, said to have had some German training. His political adviser is Mao Dsu Tung, a gifted and fanatical young man of 35 suffering from an incurable disease. This pair have made themselves into something of a legend, and the Communist High Command is invariably referred to as Chu-Mao...

'We stood up and bowed. Chiang Kaishek motioned us to sit down. I said that China was the only country whose armies were actively and continuously engaging the forces of Bolshevism in the field, and that the world's interest in China would be stimulated by first-hand information about what was happening. How soon did he expect to see the Red areas cleared up and the problem of communism in China solved? Chiang Kaishek replied, rather perfunctorily, that the Red Armies at present in the field would be wiped out by that winter; after that would come the rehabilitation of the Communist areas, for which he had already drafted plans.

'How is the situation going to develop? Is Communism a menace to the well-being of China as a whole? I doubt it. I do not think that Communism will ever be stamped out by Chinese armies, for the country is too difficult and the Reds too strong. The infection has been localized, and the probability is that for many years the same disproportionate efforts will have to be made to prevent it spreading.'

Peter Fleming, 'One's Company – a Journey to China', 1934.

SOURCE B

'By 1934 Red China occupied an important place on the map of China. It had a Marxist university and an official capital at Shuikin, in Kiangsi province, but the soviets had not yet conquered the industrial strongholds.

'Chiang Kaishek sent six expeditions against Soviet China. Each one failed, disgracefully if Bela Kun's evidence is to be believed: "The sixth expedition of Chiang Kaishek, the plan for which was worked out by General von Seeckt and two other German generals, has failed disgracefully. The Red Armies of China have grown immensely. According to bourgeois sources the number of soldiers in the regular units of the Chinese Red Army rose from 200,000 in 1932 to 350,000 persons.'

'It is still too early to predict the future of Chinese Communism, but when we remember the great passive force which China has shown in strikes and boycotts and the great active force displayed by the Kuomintang in its Russian phase, 1925–7, we must admit that it is not improbable that in a form of Communism modulated to the Chinese tradition China will find a way out of its present anarchy.'

J. Hampden Jackson, 'The Post-War World: A Short Political History, 1918–1934', 1935. Bela Kun was a Hungarian Communist who briefly ruled Hungary as a Soviet in 1919. He was a leading member of the Comintern.

EVIDENCE

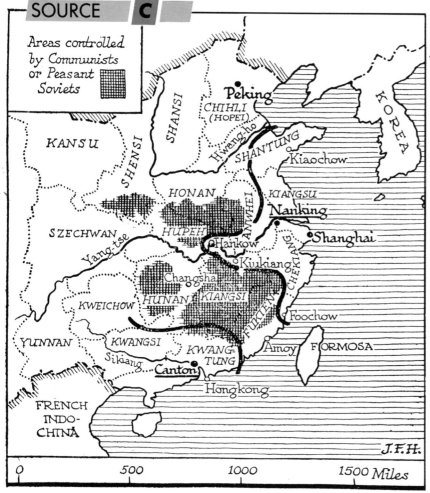

SOURCE **C**

Areas controlled by Communists or Peasant Soviets

◀ *The map included in J. Hampden Jackson's book.*

EXERCISE

1 How can you explain the differences between Sources C and D?

2 Are Sources C and D primary or secondary sources? Give reasons for your answer.

3 a What access to information about events in China did Peter Fleming have?
  b What access to information about events in China did J. Hampden Jackson have?

4 Do you think Peter Fleming is biased in favour of or against the Chinese Communists? Give reasons for your answer.

5 Do you think J. Hampden Jackson is biased in favour of or against the Chinese Communists? Give reasons for your answer.

6 Which of these two authors do you think a historian would regard as more reliable? Explain your answer.

7 Fleming and Hampden Jackson were writing at almost the same time as the events they were describing. Do you think this sort of contemporary history has special problems? Explain your answer.

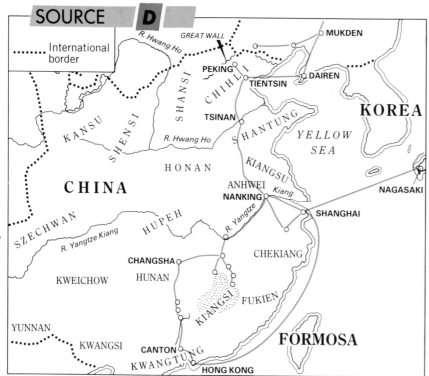

SOURCE **D**

International border

◀ *A section of the map from Peter Fleming's book, showing his route from Mukden (at that time part of the Japanese puppet state 'Manzhougou') through China and then home via Japan. The dotted area represents 'Red China'.*

3.3 THE LONG MARCH TO YANAN, 1934–5

The Long March, 1934–5.

Chiang appeases Japan

Chiang Kaishek had subdued the warlords and was managing to hold his Republic of China together. He dismissed the internal challenge of the Communists as a local 'bandit problem' which would soon be sorted out. But he now had to take account of another threat from outside China.

Foreseeing that a strong Chinese government might wish to recover Japan's extensive holdings in **Manchuria**, in 1931 **Japan** staged an excuse to conquer the province and set up the puppet state of **Manzhouguo**. In 1933 Japan also seized the adjoining province of Jehol. Japanese soldiers now peered over the Great Wall, so to speak, threatening Beijing and the whole of north China (see map).

Several of Chiang's generals wanted to resist the invaders. But Chiang held them in check and humbly negotiated a truce with Japan. He had decided that he must deal with the 'bandit problem' (which he privately knew to be more than that) before facing up to the foreign enemy. As he put it: 'The Japanese are a disease of the skin; the Communists are a disease of the heart.'

Later events proved Chiang's diagnosis to be correct: eventually the Japanese were driven off, but the patient 'died' of Communism. In the 1930s the patient saw only the 'skin disease', and wanted to be cured of it. Chiang's decision not to resist the Japanese was sharply out of tune with the burning patriotism of the Chinese people. He was unwise to ignore it.

The Long March, 1934–5

Having placated the Japanese, Chiang could again concentrate on the Communists. His fifth 'extermination campaign' in the summer of 1934 was directed by a German military adviser, **General von Seeckt**, who ordered new tactics. Guomindang forces organized a tight blockade, encircling the Jiangxi soviet, and began to close in, step by step. On the Communist side, the

SOURCE A

SOURCE B

The Long March passed through some of the most difficult terrain in China. ▲

◀ The Japanese army moves into Manchuria, September 1931.

SOURCE C

'The Long March started on 16 October 1934 from southern Jiangxi. The marchers formed an extraordinary serpent of soldiers, peasants, women, children, mules and donkeys. They had stripped their former base and, to begin with, carried their possessions. As the going became tougher they had to abandon weapons, ammunition, machinery and even silver. . .

'In June 1935 they still had to travel over 2,000 miles over terrible country. North of the Dadu river they had to climb 16,000 feet over the Great Snow Mountains. The cold was vicious and the thin mountain air made breathing difficult for those unused to the high altitude. Many perished. In July the survivors halted for three weeks to rest and recuperate. Before them stretched vast grasslands, wet, swampy and desolate. For ten days they saw no human habitation. It rained unceasingly, and they had neither firewood nor trees for shelter. In some places anyone who stepped off the narrow track was drowned in slime. Yaks were used to carry the supplies. When food became scarce they were killed and the marchers kept alive by eating yak meat and wild herbs. Finally, in October 1935 they reached northern Shaanxi. The year-long march was over.'

Hugh Higgins, 'From Warlords to Red Star', 1968.

Comintern leaders instructed the Red Army to abandon mobile warfare and to hold fixed positions. This caused such heavy losses that it was decided to evacuate the Jiangxi base. In October 1934 close to 90,000 Communists walked stealthily through the GMD noose in darkness and began the **Long March** to a new base in the north-western province of **Shaanxi** (see map).

The Long March was a remarkable feat of human endurance (see Source C and pages 22–3). Despite their severe losses, the retreat to Shaanxi was a forward step for the Communists. During a pause at the town of **Zunyi**, in January 1935, the Party rejected the leadership of the twenty-eight Bolsheviks and their Comintern advisers. Mao Zedong was elected head of the CCP. From now on he would decide the course of the Revolution.

The Communists in Yanan

At the Shaanxi base, centred on the town of **Yanan**, Mao developed a form of peasant Communism suited to Chinese conditions. Here he wrote his own rulebook of Marxism-Maoism and taught thousands of eager disciples to practise what he preached. Yanan was the birthplace of Communist China.

With a mini-state to administer, the Communist **cadres** (officials and organizers) learned skills they would later use to run the People's Republic. They organized land reform and set up schools, shops and youth groups. Teams of actors and dancers carried the Communist message to outlying villages. Peasants were taught better farming methods. Red Army recruits were taught to read. The GMD's blockade of the area forced the Communists to develop small industries to provide essentials like clothing, paper and coal. Professional skills were contributed by middle-class refugees from GMD-controlled areas.

Chiang Kaishek continued his obsessive war against the Reds. But by 1936 the 'skin disease' was getting worse: Japan was obviously preparing a full-scale war against China. For some time the CCP had been calling for a new 'united front' against the foreign threat. In Shaanxi, now much closer to the expected theatre of war, they stepped up their propaganda on this theme. The generals in charge of Chiang's campaign in Shaanxi were converted by the Communist slogan that at this moment of national crisis 'Chinese must not fight Chinese'. By agreement with the Yanan leaders, they only pretended to fight them.

In December 1936 Chiang went to Xian in Shaanxi to investigate this go-slow campaign. In what became known as the **Xian incident**, he was taken prisoner by his own generals, who brought the Communist **Zhou Enlai** from Yanan to negotiate with Chiang. These negotiations resulted in the second **United Front** between the GMD and the CCP, sealed by agreements in 1937.

Chiang ended his anti-Communist war and recognized the CCP's local authority in the 'north-west border region', although he continued to blockade it. After a decade of civil war China was now officially united under Chiang Kaishek's leadership, but both parties knew that this was only a truce in their contest to rule China.

3.4 CROSSING THE LUDING BRIDGE

EVIDENCE

Eyewitness accounts are not always accurate or reliable, even a few hours after the events they describe. But the kind of research known as **oral history**, drawn from the memory of those who took part, is sometimes the only way to reconstruct events which have left us few written records.

This is the case with the Red Army's legendary **Long March** of 1934–5. What really happened? The American writer Edgar Snow interviewed survivors at the Communist base in Yanan in 1936. Historians can refer to the story of the March in his book *Red Star over China*, published in 1937.

The March was studded with feats of daring and endurance. One of the most exciting events recorded by Edgar Snow was the capture and crossing of the **Luding Bridge** over the Dadu river on 29 May 1935. In later years this victory was often portrayed in the paintings and drama of the People's Republic.

In 1984 another American, Harrison Salisbury, retraced thousands of miles of the Red Army's route and found many survivors, now in their seventies and eighties. His book on the Long March also includes a dramatic account of the Luding Bridge crossing.

The bridge was built in 1701 across a deep and dangerous torrent, a triumph of early Chinese engineering. Harrison Salisbury tells us that in 1984 it was 'still giving good service, though closed to cart and animal traffic now'.

'Crossing the Luding Bridge' – a painting from the People's Republic in the 1950s. ▶

SOURCE  A

'Sixteen heavy iron chains, with a span of some 100 yards or more, were stretched across the river, their ends embedded on each side under great piles of cemented rock, beneath the stone bridgeheads. Thick boards lashed over the chains made the road of the bridge, but upon their arrival the Reds found that half this wooden flooring had been removed, and before them only the bare iron chains swung to a point midway in the stream.

'No time was to be lost. The bridge must be captured before enemy reinforcements arrived. Once more volunteers were called for. One by one Red soldiers stepped forward to risk their lives, and, of those who offered themselves, thirty were chosen. Hand grenades and pistols were strapped to their backs, and soon they were swinging out above the boiling river, moving hand over hand, clinging to the iron chains. Red machine-guns barked at the enemy blockades and spattered the bridgehead with bullets. The enemy replied with machine-gunning of its own, and snipers shot at the Reds tossing high above the water, working slowly towards them. The first warrior was hit, and dropped into the current below; a second fell, and then a third…

'At last one Red crawled up over the bridge flooring, uncapped a grenade and tossed it with perfect aim into the enemy refuge. Desperate, the officers ordered the rest of the planking to be torn up. It was already too late. More Reds were crawling into sight. Paraffin was thrown on the planking, and it began to burn. By then about twenty Reds were moving forward on their hands and knees, tossing grenade after grenade into the enemy machine-gun nest.

'For their distinguished bravery the heroes of Anshunchang and Luding Bridge were awarded the Gold Star, the highest decoration in the Red Army of China.'

The account by Edgar Snow, from interviews with witnesses and survivors in 1936.

SOURCE B

SOURCE C

'The thirteen iron chains are made of large links, as thick as a rice bowl, the iron hand-smelted over charcoal. Nine chains form the floor of the bridge, with two chains on either side to steady man or cart.

'Now began a military operation which would become a legend. Commissar Yang Changwu of the vanguard Fourth Regiment of the Second Division of the First Army, hero of that legend, was in 1984 a fine-looking man at 70. He had told the story many times but delighted in it. He waved three long slender fingers to drive home a point and consulted his book, *Memories of the Long March*, for a date or two.

'Twenty-two men led by Captain Liao Dazhu made the assault. Each carried a tommy-gun or a pistol, a broadsword and a dozen hand grenades. They had to crawl on the great iron chains, swaying above the river. The enemy had removed the planks two-thirds across. The buglers of the Fourth Regiment sounded "Charge!" The machine-guns opened fire. The twenty-two men began to inch their perilous way across. As they advanced, flames sprung up at the opposite end. The GMD had set fire to the bridge house.

'It was a fine day. The rain had blown away. The sun was out. It was hot and the men sweated as, link by link, never looking down at the turbulent current, they advanced across the bridge. Link by link. Hand over hand. Commissar Yang watched in agony. The Third Company men, new planks in hand, began their crawl behind the assault men, putting down planks as they crawled. Ahead, the flames leaped up. The GMD had poured paraffin on the wood. But there was no stopping the assault team. On and on they went. At the far end they clambered on to the remaining flooring and charged through the smoke and flame. They fired a burst from their machine-guns as they went. As the soot-blackened Red Army men, some with clothes aflame, dashed out on to solid land, the GMD fled.

'Eighteen of the twenty-two men survived the suicide attack, came through unscathed. The heroes of Luding Bridge did not go unrecognized. Each received a new linen tunic, a notebook, a fountain pen, an enamel bowl, an enamel pan and a pair of chopsticks. "I shared in that award," General Yang Chengwu said shyly.

'It was the greatest gift the Red Army soldiers could receive – better, far, than medals of gold.'

The account by Harrison Salisbury, in his book 'The Long March: The Untold Story', from an interview in 1984 with the commissar in charge of the operation.

EXERCISE

1 a Does Source B support the account given in Source A? Explain your answer.
  b Does Source B support the account given in Source C? Explain your answer.

2 a Compare the accounts given in Sources A and C. What are the differences?
  b Do these differences mean that one source is reliable and the other is not? Give reasons for your answer.

3 The Long March was an important part of the story of the victory of Communism in China. In later years workers were often urged to copy the heroism shown on the March. Do you think this might have affected the reliability of any of these sources? Give reasons for your answer.

4 Sources A and C both relied on oral evidence. Do historians need to treat oral evidence differently from other kinds of evidence? Explain your answer.

3.5 AT WAR WITH JAPAN, 1937–45

Nationalists and Communists face the Japanese

In July 1937 **Japan** launched a general invasion of China. Chiang put up a brave defence of the Yangzi basin area – almost too brave, for he lost some of his best troops in the first weeks of the war. But the Guomindang army was no match for the Japanese war machine. Within three months **Shanghai** and **Nanjing** had fallen. A few months later the industrial centre of **Wuhan** was taken. But Chiang refused to surrender, moving his capital to the inland city of **Chongqing**, there to sit out the war until, as he expected, the United States would be drawn into the conflict to help him win it. Japanese forces occupied large areas of northern, central and coastal China, but they could not conquer the whole country (see map). With their official slogan 'Kill all, destroy all, burn all', Japanese troops behaved with terrible cruelty.

The war gave the Chinese Communists a golden opportunity to advance their own cause. The retreat of GMD local officials to Chongqing exposed large areas of China to CCP influence, while the Red Army conducted guerrilla warfare in Japanese-occupied areas. This was the ideal situation for a **'people's war'**. The Red soldiers worked with peasant militia units to blow up trains and bridges and ambush Japanese patrols. The local people saw them as brave patriots. With the added benefit of **land reform** in the 'liberated areas' surrounding Japanese-held cities, by 1945 the Communists had won the support of 100 million peasants – peope whose lives had not been changed at all by ten years of GMD rule.

By contrast, the GMD's fortunes steadily declined during the war years. The reputation of the government worsened as GMD officials in Chongqing lined their own pockets in the wartime black market. Ever-increasing prices made life very difficult for the civilian population. Chongqing was a sitting duck for merciless Japanese bombing. Chiang's troops and supporters in 'free China' were frustrated and demoralized by the waiting game he had chosen, while in occupied China the victims of Japanese atrocities felt abandoned. The popularity Chiang had earned with his early campaigns trickled away after 1938.

The GMD's American connection

Chiang was right to foresee that the war between China and Japan would not remain a local affair. Germany's aggressive policies in Europe in the 1930s, and Japan's in the Far East, led step by step to a wider conflict. The **Second World War** began in Europe in 1939 and at first went badly for the Allies; by 1940 Britain faced Germany almost alone. Then in June 1941 Germany invaded the Soviet Union, and in December 1941 Japan attacked the United States at **Pearl Harbor**. The combined military might of

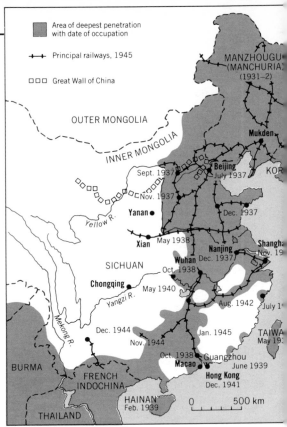

Japanese occupation of China, 1937–45.

SOURCE **A**

A street in Shanghai after a Japanese raid.

Madame Chiang with her husband and General Stilwell. Their relations were not so harmonious as this picture suggests.

the USA and the USSR eventually won the war for the Allies, but there were still three and a half years of bitter fighting ahead in several theatres of war.

The '**China Theatre**' was mainly the United States' concern. During the 1930s the government of **President F.D. Roosevelt** was following a policy of **isolationism** (trying to stay out of what were seen as other people's quarrels) and gave China very little aid at first. In fact from 1937 to 1939 it was the Soviet Union which sent Chiang's United Front government substantial military aid, hoping to keep aggressive Japan tied up in China at a time when the USSR was facing possible attack from Germany in the west. Once the Soviet Union was at war with Germany, Soviet aid to China ceased. The USSR took no further part in the war against Japan until the final days of the conflict, in 1945. On the other hand, in March 1941 the United States began a generous programme of **Lend-Lease** aid to the anti-Fascist allies, including China. After Pearl Harbor, when the USA became locked in all-out war with Japan, the 'China theatre' became very important.

The United States now tried hard to get Chiang to resist the Japanese effectively. Vast amounts of military aid were sent to Chongqing by a dangerous air route over high mountains, because by 1942 Japan had cut off land routes to China. The American **General Stilwell**, known as 'Vinegar Joe', was assigned to Chongqing to co-ordinate anti-Japanese campaigns in China and south-east Asia. Chiang gladly accepted US aid; but, to Stilwell's fury, he was reluctant to use it against the Japanese, preferring to stockpile the arms for later use against the Communists. Stilwell and Chiang came to dislike each other intensely. In 1944, at Chiang's request, Roosevelt recalled Stilwell.

Stilwell had wanted Chiang to lift his blockade of Communist areas and to join forces with theirs in one energetic anti-Japanese campaign. Other United States officials in China were equally impressed with the Communists' war effort and were ready to overlook their 'Redness' at a time when any effective anti-Fascist fighter was a welcome ally. It was even suggested that US aid might be better used if it were sent to Yanan instead of to Chongqing. But Chiang vetoed this idea and clung tightly to his pipeline of US support, helped in this regard by his American-educated wife. **Madame Chiang** was well known in the USA, and through radio broadcasts and visits there she helped to build up a favourable image of Chiang as the democratic saviour of China.

Nevertheless some influential Americans – and increasing numbers of moderate Chinese – were beginning to see more hope for China's future in the 'agrarian reformers' in the north than in the corrupt GMD officials and their hangers-on in Chongqing. As the war neared its end, the United States hoped to forge the GMD–CCP United Front into a permanent coalition government for post-war China.

3.6 CIVIL WAR, 1946–9

China at the end of the Second World War

The war in Europe ended in May 1945. The defeat of Japan was expected to be long and difficult, but in July the United States successfully tested the first atomic bomb. After two A-bombs, on **Hiroshima** on 6 August and **Nagasaki** on 9 August, Japan surrendered.

On 8 August Soviet troops had entered **Manchuria**. At the **Yalta Conference** in February 1945, Britain and the USA had promised Stalin that, in return for help to defeat Japan, they would recognize the Soviet claim to rights in Manchuria (control of two ports and two railways) seized by Japan from Tsarist Russia in 1905 (see pages 4–5). Stalin at once confirmed this by a treaty with Chiang Kaishek, in which he recognized Chiang's Guomindang government as the sole ruler of China, and then took advantage of Soviet occupation of Manchuria to carry away $2 billion worth of industrial equipment as 'war reparations'.

These actions annoyed the Chinese Communists, who hoped for Stalin's support in their renewed contest with the GMD for the right to rule China. (Soviet forces did help them later by handing over captured Japanese weapons to the CCP.) Like most outsiders Stalin probably underestimated the true strength of the Chinese Communists in 1945. Or perhaps, as some commentators have suggested, he preferred the idea of a weak GMD government in China to a strong CCP one.

Chiang now wanted the world to recognize the GMD as the legal government of China. He also needed help to regain control of the country. In 1945 the **United Nations** was formed to replace the pre-war League of Nations. Chiang was pleased when China was accepted as one of the **'big five'** nations which dominated the UN through the Security Council.

Within China, in the north the CCP was better placed to take over areas evacuated by the Japanese. So the US air force flew GMD troops to take over the cities of the north and east, which now became 'islands' in the 'sea' of Communist-controlled countryside. But the returned GMD officials soon showed themselves incapable of honest and efficient government. Their remaining middle-class supporters backed off in disgust, and the US government now had grave doubts about the GMD's fitness or ability to govern China alone.

Entry into the Second World War had ended the USA's long-standing policy of isolationism. As the major power in the Far East it wanted a strong and friendly China to support US policy in the region. Disturbed by signs of renewed civil war, **President Truman** sent the soldier-statesman **General Marshall** to try to form a coalition between the GMD and CCP. Marshall pressed Chiang hard to reform his government, but without success. By the autumn of 1946 the fighting between the Nationalists and Communists was out of control. The last round of the long struggle to rule China had begun.

SOURCE **A**

The first units of the PLA arrive in Nanjing, 1949.

SOURCE **B**

A GMD soldier leaves Nanjing, just ahead of the PLA's arrival. ▶

Defeat of the GMD in mainland China

At the outset of the **civil war** the Guomindang seemed sure to win. It had a stockpile of US weapons, and its army outnumbered the Communists by three to one. In the first year the GMD occupied almost all the towns and cities – even Yanan – while the Red Army (now renamed the **People's Liberation Army**) directed its campaigns from mobile bases in the countryside. But what counted in this war was not numbers but **strategy** and **morale** (see Source C).

Chiang's main mistake was to overstretch his forces in north China and Manchuria, where the Soviet army had allowed the Communists to gain a foothold as it evacuated the province in 1946. Unwilling to surrender important cities, Chiang kept his troops strung out like beads on a necklace, connected only by a tenuous chain of supplies and communication. The PLA was content to leave these isolated garrisons shivering in their shoes while it established firm control of the countryside. By the time the PLA turned to attack each 'bead' in force, the GMD units were thoroughly demoralized and ready to surrender. Many GMD soldiers changed sides, bringing their US weapons with them; so the PLA became stronger as the war went on.

By the end of 1948 this strategy had effectively won the war. In October and November of that year Chiang lost nearly half a million of his best troops in Manchuria, and in the next four months another one and a half million surrendered or were lost. Now meeting little resistance, the PLA crossed the Yangzi River in April 1949. Civilian morale in the shrinking GMD area of south China had already collapsed, along with the economy. Foreseeing the inevitable defeat of a government which 'had lost the confidence of its own troops and its own people', the United States stopped sending aid to the GMD and left it to its fate.

On 1 October 1949, as his army approached the original GMD base of Guangzhou on the south coast, Mao Zedong declared the **People's Republic of China** in Beijing. Chiang Kaishek retreated to the island province of **Taiwan**, newly liberated from Japan, which his successors continue to rule to this day.

SOURCE C

'The Nationalists lost the war because they were badly led, followed wrong strategy, were corrupt, and lost the support of the people, including that of their own ill-treated conscripts. The Communists won because they had a disciplined and dedicated army, were accepted as liberators by the peasantry, conceived their strategy on sound principles, and executed their operations with brilliant tactics.'

C.P. Fitzgerald in 'The History of the Twentieth Century', 1969.

CAUSATION

3.7 WHY DID THE GUOMINDANG LOSE?

The Communist victory in the Chinese civil war took the world by surprise. In 1946 all the odds seemed to favour the Guomindang, with its superior numbers and arms and the backing of the all-powerful United States. No one expected the dramatic collapse of Chiang's armies or that civilian support for his government would evaporate so quickly. Why did it happen?

There is always more than one reason for an event of such magnitude. At the moment of defeat, attention focused on recent and visible causes: Chiang's military mistakes, and the corruption and incompetence of his government under the stress of the civil war. Observers in China were shocked to see the shameful treatment of local people by GMD officials in areas just freed from Japanese rule. Many middle-class people were ruined when the currency lost its value; between 1945 and 1948 prices rose on average 30 per cent *per month*, and then soared out of control.

But historians look for long-term as well as short-term causes, and it was soon clear that the causes of the GMD's defeat lay further back. There had been a massive shift of public opinion during the period of the Japanese war. In 1937 Chiang was a national hero with the whole country behind him; while Mao Zedong was a little-known 'bandit', ruling perhaps 2 million peasants in the north-western hills. In 1945 Chiang's government and army still *looked* strong, but in reality many of the GMD's supporters had begun to doubt whether it was fit to govern China, or could ever become so. On the other hand, Mao's Red Army had grown from 50,000 to 1 million, backed up by 2.5 million peasant militia. And the Communists had won the support of 100 million peasants who were longing for change.

Some historians think that the Japanese war was *the* deciding factor which sealed the fate of the GMD regime. If there had been no war, they argue, Chiang would have stayed in power and might eventually have carried out the liberal-democratic reforms that China needed. Others believe that his regime was bound to fail in the long run for other reasons. The sources here will help you to make up your own mind about these questions.

SOURCE A

'Such misgovernment, so little regard for the citizen, so little care for the country, had fully alienated the educated class. The universities were suffering the heavy hand of the secret police. Sudden and secret arrests, mysterious disappearances, assassinations . . . The Chinese people groaned under a regime Fascist in every quality except efficiency. The Guomindang had long lost the peasants; now they had cast away their only asset, the support of the scholars.'

C. P. Fitzgerald, 'Revolution in China', 1952.

SOURCE B

'Over the years Chiang has alienated every economic group in China – peasants, workers, businessmen, and even his own soldiers. He has refused to undertake land reforms, has been unable to establish a sound currency and is leader of an incompetent and corrupt civil service and army. All these things have combined to deliver China into the waiting arms of the Communists.'

The Shanghai correspondent of an American journal, 1948.

SOURCE C

'International Communists worked overtime to turn American public opinion and diplomacy against the Chinese Government. Such adjectives as "corrupt", "incompetent", "reactionary" and "dictatorial" were flung at our government and on me personally. Their aim was to sabotage relations between China and the USA so as to enable the Chinese Communists to seize power. This was Moscow's plot, but few could see it at the time.'

Chiang Kaishek's view of why he lost, written in 1957.

CAUSATION

SOURCE D

December 1948: queueing in Shanghai for a gold allowance from the GMD government when prices had rocketed.

SOURCE E

'In spite of great losses the Nationalist forces at the end of 1947 were still twice as numerous as their opponents, and still had total control of the air. Everyone already knew that whereas the Communist forces were superbly disciplined, and treated the population with scrupulous honesty and fairness, the Nationalist forces were allowed and encouraged to loot and plunder so as to live off the country.'

C. P. Fitzgerald writing in 'History of the Twentieth Century', 1969.

SOURCE G

'To this writer the single most important cause for the downfall of the Nationalists was the eight-year Japanese war, which completely exhausted the government militarily, financially and spiritually.'

Immanuel C. Y. Hsü, 'The Rise of Modern China', 1970.

SOURCE F

'Their defeat would have been inevitable even without a Japanese invasion. The main point was their attitude to the peasants – in those days nearly 90 per cent of the country. And they couldn't solve the peasant question – that is, giving land to the peasants – because their main support came from the landlords, who naturally wanted to hang on to their land.'

Jack Chen in a BBC radio programme, 1978.

EXERCISE

1 Look carefully at each source and make a list of all the suggested causes for the GMD's defeat.
   a Which causes are indicated in more than one source?
   b Which causes affected the majority of peasants?
   c Which causes affected the educated class?
   d Were any of these causes due to circumstances beyond the GMD's control?
   e Were any of them the GMD's 'fault', which it could have corrected?

2 Now arrange your list in a 'ladder of importance'. Causes which you consider equally important may occupy the same 'rung'. Explain the particular order of importance you have decided on.

3 From your own knowledge of this period, do you think any of the causes suggested in the sources are untrue? Explain your answer.

4 Do you think the GMD's defeat was inevitable? Give reasons for your answer.

4.1 EARLY YEARS OF THE PEOPLE'S REPUBLIC, 1949–56

China and the cold war

In 1949 China 'stood up', in Mao Zedong's words, after a century of weakness and exploitation by foreigners. Millions of Chinese hoped that a strong and independent China would be respected and welcomed by the international community. These hopes were cancelled out by events in neighbouring Korea.

The Second World War was scarcely over before the two former allies, the USA and USSR, began to oppose each other in a **cold war** of fear and suspicion. Faced with a strong Communist state which many people in the West thought was out to dominate the world, the United States resolved on a policy of **containment**: Communism must be 'contained' in the area it already held. This became the main aim of US post-war foreign policy.

War in Korea

In February 1950 the new People's Republic of China (PRC) signed a **Treaty of Friendship** with the Soviet Union. For some Americans this confirmed that Mao was just a puppet of Stalin, who had taken over China as part of Moscow's plan of world conquest. They saw further evidence of a conspiracy between Stalin and Mao in the **Korean War**.

In 1945 the former Japanese colony of Korea had been divided into a Communist North and a more or less democratic South. In January 1950 North Korea invaded South Korea in an attempt to reunite the country. **President Truman** sent the US navy to help South Korea and organized a **United Nations** rescue force under the American **General MacArthur**. As MacArthur's army pushed the North Koreans back towards the Chinese frontier, China sent in thousands of troops to help the North Koreans drive the UN and US forces back into South Korea.

The Korean War ended in 1953 with the country still divided into North and South. But the North Korean invasion and China's intervention in the war were now seen in the West as a planned attack on the 'free world' that the United States had undertaken to protect from Communism. So Washington renewed its support of the **Guomindang**, now confined to **Taiwan**, as the legal government-in-exile of all China. The USA banned trade with mainland China and encircled it with a ring of military alliances. The US government used its influence in the United Nations to prevent the Beijing government from taking over China's seat.

Cut off from the Western world, China had to rely entirely on the Soviet Union for help with its economic development.

China's economic recovery

The new Communist government was careful not to make enemies of the Chinese middle class whose skills were needed to run the country. Former GMD officials worked on under the direction of CCP cadres. In a year or two the **economic framework** of the new state was established. In 1953 the first **Five-Year Plan** began a programme of industrialization under Soviet guidance, with a loan of $3 billion and thousands of Soviet technicians to help construct the large industrial plants China needed.

Chinese Communists being taken prisoner by US Marines during fighting in North Korea.

SOURCE **B**

Land reform and collectivization

During the 1950s the system of **landholding** and **work methods** were transformed throughout China in a step-by-step process. Mao insisted on lenient treatment of the hard-working richer peasants; he wanted to avoid Stalin's mistakes in the Soviet Union, where the brutal enforcement of collective agriculture in the 1930s had caused a terrible famine and hatred of the government.

The **Land Reform Law of 1950** extended to the whole country what had been practised in Communist areas before 1949. The first task of the land reform team was to survey the land and classify the villagers on a social scale from landlord through 'rich', 'middle' and 'poor' peasants down to landless labourers. Debts were immediately cancelled and rents reduced. Then came the transfer of surplus land and other possessions from the top two categories to the bottom two, leaving the former gentry families with just enough to live on and the situation of most 'middle' families unchanged.

For millions of downtrodden peasants, land reform was the heart of the Chinese Revolution, the moment when each man and woman 'stood up' to face their own personal enemy, the landlord. At **People's Courts** and **'speak bitterness' meetings** they were deliberately encouraged to spit out their rage and pent-up hatred against the local 'tyrant' who had raped his tenants' wives, seized their land for unpaid debts and hoarded grain at times of famine. About one million landlords and other 'bad elements' were executed or lynched on the spot as the peasants took their revenge for the uncountable crimes of past centuries (see pages 32–3).

Land reform at last fulfilled Sun Yatsen's goal of 'land to the tiller' (see pages 12–3). But however fair the original share-out, differences of wealth and status would soon increase as larger or harder-working families bought up neighbouring land. It was also essential to increase agricultural output, and the government believed that this could only be achieved by pooling the peasants' labour, tools and animals in larger farming units where machinery and new methods could be introduced.

Collectivization Peasants were not to be forced but would be gently coaxed into co-operative farming. First, **mutual-aid teams** were formed, with seven to ten households sharing their tools, labour and draught animals and working each family's land separately. The next step was to set up **lower-stage co-operatives** of thirty to forty households in which the land was collectively farmed but still individually owned, and profits were shared accordingly. Only with the third step of **higher-stage co-operatives** did the peasants move into a 'truly socialist' system of collective work and landownership. By 1956 these units of three to four hundred families had been organized almost everywhere in China.

A Poor Peasant League measuring out land for redistribution in 1949. ▼

4.2 LAND REFORM IN YELLOW EARTH VILLAGE

EMPATHY

When he was a student in London, Esther Cheo Ying's father met and married a hotel chambermaid and returned with her to Shanghai. Esther was born in 1932. Her parents' marriage was unhappy, so in 1938, her mother returned to England with her three children. At 15 Esther managed to renew contact with her father in Shanghai. Despised in England as a 'Chinky' she felt herself to be more Chinese than English and longed to return 'home'.

The chance came when she met a Chinese pilot in London. They married and set off for China in 1948. But in Hong Kong they parted, she to join the People's Liberation Army in Beijing, her husband to join the GMD in Taiwan.

Although they corresponded and spoke on the telephone, Esther's hoped-for reunion with her father never took place. As one of the 'bourgeoisie' (middle class) he was having a hard time, though just surviving, in Communist China. After a spell in the army, Esther worked for Radio Beijing, and later as an interpreter. Taking advantage of the new Marriage Law she divorced her Chinese husband and later married a British Communist journalist based in Beijing. Gradually they both grew tired of the endless political campaigns of Maoist China. They resented the unspoken hostility towards foreigners of many of their Chinese comrades. By the time her husband was re-assigned to Europe, Esther had realized that after all she was more English than Chinese, and she gratefully returned to live in England.

These years of Esther Cheo Ying's life are described in her book *Black Country Girl in Red China* (1980). The extracts here relate her experiences as part of a PLA land-reform team in Yellow Earth Village, twenty-five miles north of Beijing, in 1949.

Esther Cheo Ying as a PLA soldier.

SOURCE A

'Kuang, the local tyrant, was finally brought to be "struggled against" by the peasants. He managed to instil fear even though he stood there humbled. Gradually people got up, and at first there were timid requests that he return grain and possessions he had taken in lieu of unpaid rents. As the others saw that Kuang was powerless to retaliate they too plucked up courage and began to accuse him.

'I listened to peasants come forward and accuse old Kuang of cruelty and viciousness of a kind which I did not feel possible from such a kindly looking old gentleman. But it was difficult not to believe weeping women who tore their clothes off to show terrible scars. One could not fail to be convinced when one woman described how her baby was torn in half because she would not sleep with old Kuang. His defence was: "Well, you should not have encouraged me. You took my present."

'As the day wore on, the crowd became angrier until hysteria broke out and they had to be restrained by armed soldiers from lynching old Kuang on the spot.'

Old Kuang stands before his accusers at the 'struggle meeting'.

EMPATHY

SOURCE D

'Part of my strengthening process was to attend the public execution where 200 landlords and notorious members of underground secret societies were to be shot. I still have nightmares about it. The victims were kneeling down beside cheap deal coffins, their hands tied behind their backs with wire. About six security police nonchalantly moved along, shooting them in the back of the head. As they fell, some of their heads split open, some just fell with a neat little hole, while others had their brains splattered all over the dusty ground and on to the clothes of other victims.

'Wang T'ao, who had come along in his jeep to supervise, saw me turn away in revulsion and start running. He chased after me, grabbed me by the shoulders and shouted: "Take a good look. This is what the revolution is all about!"

'At our follow-up meeting I said it made me sick. I asked what sort of person was needed to calmly go around and shoot others in cold blood? I was accused of having the wrong class attitude; my revolutionary fervour was not strong enough. The men who carried out the executions were ridding the country of vermin. I was asked "What would your reactions be if you were faced with the same situation as some of the peasant women had faced in the past?" I tried to argue that there was a difference between revenge and cold-blooded murder. I supposed if my baby had been torn in half I might have cheered to see the murderer shot. I was shouted down by hysterical men and women, the spit flying from the corners of their mouths, accusing me of being in sympathy with the enemies of the people, until I put my hands over my ears and pleaded: "I'm sorry, I'm sorry! Help me to understand."'

SOURCE E

The struggle meeting – a new year wall poster in 1950.

SOURCE F

'It was while we were engaged in land reform that the harshness of the times touched us directly. One night, an ex-landlord crept into the temple where some of the men of our group were sleeping and slit the throats of four of them before another woke up and gave the alarm. Seeing these young dead soldiers who had walked with us in the lanes to protect us, who had joked with us, and one who had taught me to turn the heel of a sock I was knitting, I could have shot that particular landlord myself.'

EXERCISE

1 Why did the peasants' attitude towards Old Kuang change as the struggle meeting went on (Source A)?

2 Some of Esther's comrades in the land-reform team were peasants from other villages. Do you think they would have reacted differently at the struggle meeting? Give reasons for your answer.

3 Why do you think the PLA made Esther and other young recruits witness the executions in Beijing (Source D)?

4 Why could Esther not bear to watch the mass execution, yet in the village she 'could have shot that particular landlord myself' (Sources D and F)?

5 Why do you think the new year poster of 1950 portrayed a 'struggle meeting' (Source E)?

4.3 SOCIAL REFORMS AND POLITICAL CAMPAIGNS, 1949–57

The new government swept through all the dusty and sordid corners of social life in Old China. Opium dens and brothels were closed, and their inhabitants were 'reformed'. Corrupt business people and bureaucrats were weeded out for punishment. **Public health campaigns** tackled widespread diseases and the high infant mortality rate. More **schools** were opened, and a start was made on the huge problem of **illiteracy** (in 1949 at least 80 per cent of the population was illiterate).

The status of women
Among the most important of these reforms were those to regulate **family life** and improve the **situation of women** (See pages 36–7). In Guomindang China the status of middle-class women had been considerably raised, but for peasant women almost nothing had changed by 1949 except that the cruel practice of foot-binding had died away.

The **Marriage Law of 1950** placed women legally on an equal basis with men. It prohibited child marriage, matchmaking for money and other practices of Old China, and it carefully laid down the rights of women and children. Other regulations provided for equal pay and maternity benefits, and for child care at the workplace, to enable women to work outside the home. The overall aim of these changes was to break the power of the traditional male-dominated family which had kept women in subjection.

In Old China the family had been the focus of personal loyalty. Now the Communist Party wanted everyone to feel part of a wider national community and give their loyalty to 'the people' as a whole. This was part of a general campaign to encourage socialist ways of thinking in Mao's China.

Thought reform
For the CCP it was not enough just to build a society in which property and wealth would be communally owned and enjoyed. Even more important was the task of creating a **'new socialist man'** (and woman too, of course) to live in it. They must be unselfish people who would freely give their talents and labour to the community and expect only an equal share of the money and goods produced by their combined efforts. They must learn to 'serve the people' rather than their own self-interest.

In the early 1950s the government introduced a programme of 'ideological remoulding' or **thought reform**. This was intended to prepare the Chinese people for the future Communist utopia. Lessons and 'struggle meetings' were held in every school and workplace to study the **Thought of Mao Zedong** and persuade people to cast out the selfish thoughts and habits of their upbringing (see pages 38–9).

The conversion process was fairly successful with people of little education who had personally benefited under the new regime. It was not very hard to convince them that they owed

One important aim of the government was primary education for all.

their good fortune to the ideas of Marx and Chairman Mao. But China's several million intellectuals – teachers, artists, writers and philosophers – had lost wealth and status in the new society. Many were Western-educated and would not accept the crude slogans of Party propaganda. Yet the Party believed these people carried into New China the 'dangerous' Confucian attitudes of Old China, a distaste for manual labour and contempt for uneducated people. If their thoughts were not 'reformed' they would pass on these attitudes to the younger generation.

In 1956 events in the outside world prompted the CCP to risk a public argument with China's left-over bourgeoisie. After Stalin's death in 1953 his successor **Khrushchev** had to deal with rebellions against Soviet control in Eastern Europe and simmering discontent in the Soviet Union. In 1956 Khrushchev astonished the world by admitting that Stalin was a cruel tyrant who had ruthlessly crushed all opposition to his policies. He now promised to 'de-Stalinize' the Soviet system.

These events were embarrassing for all Communists, and a warning for China. Mao decided to lift the lid of Party control to see what opposition might be lurking underneath and to show the world that Mao's China was not like Stalin's Russia. He was also worried about arrogant Party cadres seeking privileges for themselves just like old-style government officials. They had to be reminded that their job was to serve the masses, not to lord it over them.

The Hundred Flowers campaign

In 1956–7 China's press and other media were opened up to **'let a hundred flowers bloom'**, as the Chinese put it – in other words, to allow free discussion and criticism of the government and its work. The invitation was mainly addressed to the educated classes. Many educated people had stood on the sidelines up to now, but were sure to be impressed, the Party leaders thought, by the progress made since 1949. This hope proved to be mistaken.

The government was taken aback by the torrent of hostile comment that resulted. People not only complained about particular policies, but questioned the whole socialist framework of New China. The Party had expected constructive criticism, but this was counter-revolution! The Hundred Flowers campaign was abruptly ended and replaced by an **'anti-Rightist campaign'** in which many of the critics who had publicly identified themselves were sent to 'reform their thinking' through manual labour. Understandably, the victims concluded that this had been the real purpose behind the invitation to speak out freely.

Ten years later these unreformed 'Rightists' would be singled out again for even worse persecution. But in the meantime Mao turned his attention to problems in the economy.

◀ *Political posters on a gateway in Beijing.*

CHANGE

4.4 PROGRESS FOR WOMEN IN NEW CHINA

SOURCE A

'*Article 1* Polygamy, concubinage, child betrothal and the exaction of money or gifts in connection with marriage shall be prohibited. *Article 2* Marriage shall be based on the complete willingness of the two parties. No third party shall be allowed to interfere…
Article 17 Divorce shall be granted when husband and wife both desire it.'

Extracts from the Marriage Law of 1950.

SOURCE B

'There was a rash of divorces following the 1950 Marriage Law, and on 29 September 1951 the *People's Daily* reported 21,433 divorce cases, 76.6 per cent of which had been brought by women… Now divorce is relatively rare, we were told. "Why would people want to be divorced when they married of their own volition?"'

Ruth Sidel, 'Women and Child Care in China – A Firsthand Report', 1972. This writer is a specialist in women and children's welfare.

SOURCE C

'In one commune in Shaanxi, there were 146 girls under the age of 5 who were betrothed, accounting for 43 per cent of their age group. Among 5- to 10-year-olds, 81 per cent were engaged. A number of Chinese women I met complained more bitterly about their trouble in getting a divorce than about anything else. "The Party secretary wouldn't say why we had been refused" Guiying told me, "but I think personally it is a matter of face. The authorities are very feudal. Divorce to them is still immoral."'

Fox Butterfield, 'China – Alive in the Bitter Sea', 1982. The author was the 'New York Times' correspondent in China in the early 1980s.

Middle-class women like Qiu Jin (see pages 8–9) began to receive legal rights and wider opportunities under the Guomindang. But the GMD reforms for women, like other GMD laws, had little effect outside the cities. It was left to the Communists to liberate China's vast number of enslaved peasant women.

Jack Belden, in his book *China Shakes the World* (1949), tells the story of an illiterate peasant girl he met in 1948. Like so many others, Gold Flower was married against her will to an older man who was very cruel to her. During the civil war she left the husband she hated and, with her sisters in the Communist women's association, helped to organize resistance to the GMD armies. Then they began to overthrow the traditional power of men in their village – not only the landlords and money-lenders, but their own husbands and fathers-in-law. Through this self-liberating process Gold Flower ceased to be an 'inside person' confined to the house as a virtual slave, and became A PERSON in village life.

Unlike Qiu Jin, executed for her revolutionary activities in 1907, Gold Flower lived to see women's liberation in China officially endorsed by the Communists' Marriage Law of 1950. Since then, educated professional women have advanced even further, in some ways, than their counterparts in the West. Today nearly half China's doctors are women, and a third of scientists and engineers. At this level a woman may receive equal pay for equal work, and she is well served with child-care facilities and maternity benefits.

But how have Gold Flower's daughters and granddaughters fared in New China? Mao's saying that 'Women hold up half the sky' is often cited to show the Chinese Communist Party's commitment to women's rights. Yet feudal customs and attitudes are not abolished overnight, or even in thirty-five years. Western visitors have reported on the situation of women at various times during the last few decades, as the peasants have moved from family farming to the commune system and back again to family farming in the 1980s. Sources A to C concern **marriage and divorce**, Sources E to H **equality at work.**

SOURCE D

CHANGE

SOURCE E

'Women enjoy equal rights with men in all spheres of political, economic, cultural, social and family life. Men and women enjoy equal pay for equal work.'

Article 53 of China's Constitution.

SOURCE F

'Women now no longer work just in the house; they also work in the fields and earn their own money. But the men of the older generation still say: "What does a woman know? Women know nothing! What's a woman worth? Women are worth nothing!" In such families the men decide everything and their wives say: "We are just women. We are not allowed to say anything."'

Complaint from women villagers recorded by the Swedish writer Jan Myrdal in 'Report from a Chinese village', 1963. Myrdal and his wife lived in a northern Chinese village for a month in 1962.

SOURCE G

'Lihua recalled that in her village girls were not sent to school at all, for their parents still regard them as "outsiders". At marrriage, they will move away. Girl babies in her village are called "a thousand ounces of gold"; but a boy is called "ten thousand ounces of gold".

'In the communes women are usually given the most back-breaking labour, transplanting rice or picking beans, while their menfolk are off driving tractors or acting as cadres. An American sociologist who lived on a commune in Hebei province calculated that women actually did 80 per cent of all the fieldwork.'

Fox Butterfield, 'China – Alive in the Bitter Sea', 1982.

SOURCE H

'Chinese women's pay has in general stayed 25 per cent below that of comparable men… Deng Xiaoping's economic policies mean that the family has again become the basic unit of production and consumption in rural society. This has had two results. First, it has returned financial control to the man as "head of the family" – whereas in the communes, women's finanical share could not be denied or diverted. And second, it has meant extra work for women: the household tasks of which the commune had previously relieved them have been dumped back on them again.'

Marie-Ange Donzé, 'New Internationalist' magazine, 1987.

EXERCISE

1 Why do you think there was a 'rash of divorces' in 1951, yet relatively few in later years (Sources B and C)?

2 a How did the 1950 Marriage Law change the system for marriage?

 b Do the sources suggest that these changes were carried out?

3 a How did China's Constitution try to improve the situation of women at work?

 b Do the sources suggest that these changes have taken place?

4 Do you agree or disagree with the following statements? In each case copy the statement and then explain your reasons for agreeing or disagreeing with it.

 a There has been rapid change in the position of women since the Communists came to power in China.

 b Improvement in the position of women has been slower than the political leaders in Beijing wanted.

 c The position of women in China today suggests that the forces resisting change in Chinese society are stronger than the efforts to bring about change.

◀ *Peasant girls threshing grain on a commune.*

4.5 THOUGHT REFORM

EMPATHY

In the modern world we are all aware of **propaganda** – the presentation of biased information, or even lies, as if it is the whole truth. This happened in Hitler's Germany when the whole nation was drenched with Nazi propaganda. The results were so harmful that the Allies set up 're-education' programmes after the war to re-introduce democratic ideas into Germany.

In the **Korean War** of 1950–3 (see pages 30–1) the Chinese Communists showed the world a new kind of political indoctrination. They persuaded some United Nations prisoners to make broadcasts across the lines confessing that they were 'agents of American imperialism' who had committed 'crimes against the Chinese people' as soldiers in the UN/US army. A few of these men chose to live in China rather than go home after the war. In the West it was said they had been 'brainwashed'.

In the early 1950s the Chinese people were also being 'brainwashed' – or 're-educated', as the Communist government saw it. Mao always believed that this was a necessary part of creating a socialist society (pages 34–5). At Yanan in 1942 he had explained to Party members that people had to be rescued from their 'wrong thinking' like a patient being treated for an illness: 'Our object in exposing errors and criticizing shortcomings is like that of a doctor in curing a disease. The entire purpose is to save the person, not cure him to death'.

In the **thought reform** campaign of 1951–2 the CCP 'doctors' set to work on millions of Chinese citizens. There were two separate phases in thought reform procedure. First, the members of the group would be coaxed and bullied through **self-criticism** to recognize and confess their past misdeeds and wrong ideas, the 'evil remnants' of the old society. Each member of the group would help to interrogate the others and then submit to their own interrogation in turn. Having cleared out the 'evil remnants', he or she was ready for the second phase of **re-education** in Communist ideas. Finally the 'reborn' citizen would be expected to make some kind of pledge to 'serve the people' in New China.

SOURCE B

'Thought reform begins with light and friendly open discussion, encouraging warm group feeling. At a moment decided by the official running the meeting a particular person is subjected to intense questioning, accusation and pressure by others in the group to lay bare his "evil remnants", to repent and swear selfless service to the people in future. In this phase the target individual is made to feel guilt, shame, loss of face, loneliness and despair. Real or pretended surrender is the only way to avoid becoming an outcast.

'Arrogance, liberalism, lack of faith in the masses, contempt for physical work, wrong political thinking. To admit to these charges brings relief. More than relief, the positive sense of belonging.'

Alan Winnington's description of a thought-reform session.

SOURCE A

The British Communist, Alan Winnington was working at the New China News Agency in Beijing in 1951. Here he reports a speech by a senior CCP official to prepare the office workers for a thought-reform session.

'"Most comrades are good, but many have things they try to hide. Now is the time for those who did bad things to repent openly. We are not working in the dark. Secret agents have surrendered, others have been captured. They have confessed. We have documents, names. Isn't it better to tell the truth now than be caught in a lie? We know that Jang Pihua concealed that her father worked for the Japanese. Li Pinhong hid his father's ties with the American imperialists. Ye Zhou hid the fact that his father was rich.

'"We all come from the old corrupt society, bringing rotten morals. Do we want to carry them over into our New China? We must try to be bright new people."'

EMPATHY

SOURCE C

'I felt very confused and upset. I knew that the matter must be settled – and that if I didn't do well, the government would discover that I wasn't being frank enough and I would be in for trouble. I felt that if I could once and for all settle the turmoil in my mind, I would calm down and be able to feel that I had done my duty to my country.'

George Chen's experience of thought reform at Beijing University.

SOURCE D

'There are 470 million Chinese in New China and I am one of them. This New China is working for the interests and welfare of the people of China as well as of the world. I have no wish to be an onlooker. I want to take part in the glorious and mighty enterprises which should be participated in not only by the young, but by the people of all ages, including the old. I am now close to 60, and I am a criminal for having sinned against the people. From now on, however, I shall strive to become a new man and a teacher of the people.'

Extract from Professor Chin's confession, published in a national newspaper in China in April 1952.

SOURCE E

A thought reform session.

SOURCE F

George Chen's family had moved to Hong Kong when the Communists took over, but he chose to continue his education in Beijing. Here he describes how he felt on a visit to his family in Hong Kong.

'I found myself unaccustomed to the capitalist way of life, and could not bear the vanity, waste and extravagance of life here. I resented differences and discrimination between rich and poor, well-to-do people enslaving their servants. I thought that I could openly scorn and hate them, for I was so much superior to them.'

EXERCISE

1 The Communist leaders faced many problems when they first came to power. Why do you think they made thought reform one of their priorities?

2 How do you think the following people would have reacted to news of the thought-reform campaign? Explain your answer in each case.
   a A senior CCP official.
   b A soldier in the GMD army in Taiwan whose family was still in China.
   c A member of the old land-owning class.

3 How do you think George Chen's parents would have reacted to his political views when he visited them (Source F)?

4 Professor Chin was highly educated and had lived in the West.
   a Does this mean that his confession was not sincere? Explain your answer.
   b What considerations may have influenced his decision to confess?
   c Why do you think the CCP published his confession in a national newspaper?

4.6 THE 'GREAT LEAP' SPLITS THE PARTY, 1958–65

It was clear by the mid-1950s that Soviet-style economic development was not suitable for China. It was too centralized and rigid, and the concentration on heavy industry meant that **agriculture** and **light industry** were getting left behind. China had very little capital or expertise for high-technology projects, but Mao argued that its huge resources of **labour** could be used to build small-scale industries throughout the countryside and vast earthworks to irrigate and drain the land. These millions of peasants were as yet untrained – but never mind, argued Mao, they would learn in the best way possible, by doing! Mao always believed that 'Reds' could achieve more than 'experts'; now he wanted China to prove it.

This was the over-optimistic thinking behind a bold new economic policy which was intended to raise China's industrial and agricultural output to the level of the advanced nations. At the same time the policy would push 'the masses' into more socialist ways of living and working.

The **Great Leap Forward**, as the new policy was called, was launched in 1958 with all the usual fanfare of Chinese Communist Party campaigns. Slogans decked every wall and were carried on placards to construction sites by marching columns of workers. Six million city-dwellers helped to dig reservoirs and irrigation canals, dikes and drainage ditches. Enthusiastic cadres supervised the building of 600,000 **backyard steel furnaces**, intended as the foundation of rural industries.

To co-ordinate all these projects and organize the armies of workers, after 1958 **People's Communes** replaced the co-operative farms. The communes combined collective farming and small industries with all the functions of local government. They included up to 5,000 families grouped into **'production teams'** (one village each) and **'production brigades'** (several village teams joined together). Each family received a share of food and cash according to the number of 'work-points' earned by the adults of the household. The commune system was officially blessed by the CCP as 'the best form of organization for the attainment of Socialism and the gradual transition to Communism'.

The West (and the Soviet Union) watched the Great Leap Forward with astonishment and scorn. Could backyard steel furnaces really 'outstrip Great Britain in fifteen years', as the CCP boasted? Surely not! These doubts proved to be well-founded. Wildly exaggerated output figures were proclaimed – and then retracted. Backyard steel was useless for any industrial purpose, and the makeshift furnaces were washed away in rainstorms. Worst of all, grain was left to rot in the fields while peasants were working on construction jobs miles away. In 1959–61 at least 16 million people starved to death, and many more millions went hungry. The **famine** was made worse by floods and drought (see pages 42–3) and the abrupt ending of Soviet aid in 1960.

Massed labour on construction work during the Great Leap Forward. ▶

The Chinese–Soviet dispute

The quarrel between China and the Soviet Union had begun with an argument about future relations between the 'socialist camp' of Marxist countries and the 'capitalist camp' led by the United States. In the nuclear age, said Khrushchev in 1956, war was so dangerous that the two camps must learn to live in **peaceful coexistence** and settle their conflicts by negotiation.

The Chinese–Soviet dispute was a complicated mixture of issues (see pages 44–5). But the extreme bitterness of the quarrel in the 1960s arose from Mao's determination to convert China and the whole Communist world to his own 'pure' interpretation of Marxism. He thought that Krushchev and some leaders of the CCP were abandoning or revising the basic beliefs of Marxism and that these 'revisionist' policies must be stopped.

'Maoists' versus 'Rightists'

After the Great Leap Forward, a group of leaders including President **Liu Shaoqi** and **Deng Xiaoping** introduced more right-wing (that is, less socialist) policies to help China recover from the disaster of 1959–61. **Family farming** and **private markets** were encouraged. In **industry** cash bonuses and other financial rewards replaced the political slogans of the Great Leap as a means to encourage hard work. These measures soon had the effect of increasing food supplies and industrial output.

By the early 1960s the CCP leadership had split into **Rightists** and **Maoists**. The Rightists wanted to build up large-scale industry and update China's defences. They believed that peasants and workers would only work hard for cash rewards. They wanted a highly-trained professional class to modernize China, and for the same reason they wanted to make up the quarrel with the Soviet Union – especially when (1964–5) the United States was becoming deeply involved in the **Vietnam War** on China's doorstep.

In Mao's view these ideas would take China down the **'capitalist road'**. By this he meant the kind of halfway socialism he observed in the Soviet Union, where a 'new bourgeoisie' of Party officials and professional people enjoyed a high standard of living and privileges not shared by ordinary workers. He thought the same thing was happening in China under Rightist policies. To create the kind of socialist society he wanted, Mao believed that education and economic investment should be spread more evenly over the whole population. Above all, there must be no let-up in the effort to teach everyone to 'serve the people' instead of their own self-interest.

With Rightists in control of the government, Mao complained of being treated 'like a dead ancestor'. With Defence Minister **Lin Piao** he plotted a come-back. The *Little Red Book*, a pocket digest of Mao's thoughts, became the handbook of every soldier. And in the **Socialist Education Movement** everyone was urged to 'learn from the People's Liberation Army'. When this campaign did not correct the 'capitalist tendencies', Mao launched the whole nation into the **Great Proletarian Cultural Revolution** (see pages 46–7).

4.7 WHAT CAUSED THE THREE HARD YEARS?

CAUSATION

If all the relevant information is available, historians can usually agree about *what* happened in history, and when. A more difficult task is to sort out the *causes* of an event, especially when there are several factors to be taken into account. One such case is the controversial period of China's history known as the **Great Leap Forward**.

In 1958 the Chinese Communist Party's Central Committee under Mao's leadership launched the Great Leap Forward, a gigantic national effort to increase industrial and agricultural production. In the countryside communes were formed by joining up the existing co-operative farms into larger units. Many thousands of peasants were now engaged in building irrigation schemes and setting up rural industries, as well as farming. Their private plots, on which they had previously raised vegetables, pigs and poultry for sale in private markets, were abolished. In future all farmwork was to be communal, and the produce would be sold to the state.

The summer of 1958 was a good one, but in 1959 and 1960 there was very bad weather – floods in some areas, drought in others – which seriously affected the harvest. In the winter of 1959 there were severe food shortages. In 1960 famine struck China for the first time since the Communists had come to power. At least 16 million people starved to death in what came to be called the **three hard years** of 1959–61.

Was the famine caused by the policies of the Great Leap or by the bad weather? China's President **Liu Shaoqi** said later that the disaster was '30 per cent the fault of nature, and 70 per cent human error'. In 1961, against Mao's opposition, he brought in new economic policies which restored private plots and free markets (see pages 40–1). Food production gradually increased, but it took several years to pass the pre-Great Leap level of 1957.

SOURCE A

'Only production counted. We worked night and day to build seven extra generators. I hardly slept for a week. Then we got a Polish engine to drive the generators. It did not have enough power but they went ahead. Mao had said we can do anything. In no time the engine's bearings went. After we went through three engines we had to go back to the city electricity supply, but it could not produce enough. The machines broke down. I was taken off my work and sent to tend the steel ovens.'

A factory electrician's recollection of the Great Leap Forward.

SOURCE C

'Food became scarce in Beijing and queues built up at the few vegetable stalls. Meat was almost non-existent and the cat population rapidly declined. At a well-known Chinese artist's home I had a very passable dinner once which turned out to be a neighbour's ginger tom. With their basic needs supplied by the commune there was no encouragement for peasants to produce poultry and pigs which had brought in extra income and helped food supplies in the cities.'

A Western resident of Beijing recalls the years 1958-9.

◄ *Makeshift or 'backyard' steel furnaces built during the Great Leap Forward.*

SOURCE D

'The total grain crop for 1957 had been about 195 million tons. In 1958 the total actually increased to 200 million tons. At the time however, it was officially proclaimed that the crop had been 260 million tons. The exaggerated estimate led dining-halls in some communes to offer very generous meals, and use up most of their food stocks before the 1959 harvest came in.'

Edwin E. Moise, 'Modern China', 1986.

SOURCE E

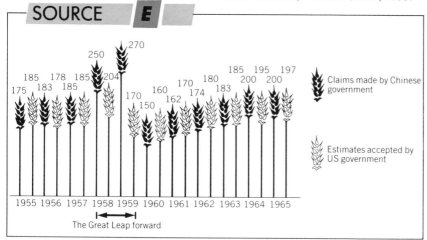

Grain production in millions of tons, 1955–65.

SOURCE F

'The official report of the Central Committee of 26 August 1959 recognized that the figures published previously for economic achievement during 1958 were exaggerated by 40 to 50 per cent. In particular, the grain harvest had been only 250 million tons. (The real figure was undoubtedly still lower.) Another bad harvest in 1959, due in part to natural calamities, but also the disorganization of the economy and the setting up of communes, led to a lean and bitter winter.'

Stuart Schram, 'Mao Zedong', 1966.

SOURCE G

'In 1959 the Great Leap began to become a disaster. People were no longer capable of the fantastic exertions of 1958. The shortage of agricultural labour was so acute that the total acreage planted in food crops was significantly below the level of 1957. Most important, the weather was disastrous. The 1959 harvest amounted to only about 170 million tons. Hunger became widespread, and some people began to starve; others went on the road as beggars.'

Edwin E. Moise, 'Modern China', 1986.

EXERCISE

1 Causes can sometimes be strung together in chains. For example, the history syllabus you are following says that you must do course work. So your teacher will tell you to do a piece of course work. The immediate cause of your doing a piece of course work is the teacher telling you to do it, but the underlying cause is the examination board's syllabus.
  a From Source B, make a chain of causation leading to the electrician being transferred to other work.
  b From Source C, make a chain of causation resulting in people eating a cat for dinner.
  c From Source D, make a chain of causation leading to food shortages in 1959.

  In each case, what was the underlying cause of what happened?

2 Study Source E.
  a Does it show the immediate cause of famine in 1959–60?
  b Does it show the underlying cause or causes? Explain your answer.

3 Compare the statements by Edwin Moise (Sources D and G) with the statement by Stuart Schram (Source F). Do you think that these authors agree with each other about the underlying causes of the famine? Give reasons for your answer.

4 Mao certainly did not intend the Great Leap Forward to result in famine and hardship. Yet it did so. Does this mean that his decision to launch the Great Leap was not a cause of the hardship that followed? Give reasons for your answer.

4.8 REASONS FOR THE CHINESE–SOVIET DISPUTE

CAUSATION

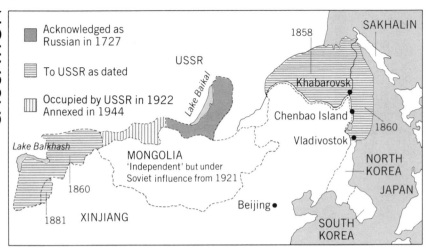

The Chinese–Soviet border.

'Until the mid-nineteenth century, Russia's main interest regarding China was to secure its Far Eastern borders. After that, Russia began to press for "special rights" in China, especially in Manchuria, Xinjiang and Korea. Frustrated by its defeat in the Russo–Japanese War, Russia from time to time tried to extend its influence in Chinese territory.'

F. Schurmann and O. Schell, 'China Readings 3: Communist China', 1967 (adapted).

SOURCE **B**

'Since Khrushchev took over, the new bourgeois elements have gradually risen to the ruling positions in the Party and government. They pocket incomes that are dozens or even 100 times those of the average Soviet worker or peasant. By promoting cash bonuses, Khrushchev is turning all human relations into money relations and encouraging individualism and selfishness.'

Statement by the Chinese Communist Party in 1964.

In 1949 most outsiders believed that the Soviet Union welcomed, and had assisted, the victory of the Chinese Communists over the Guomindang. Chinese–Soviet friendship seemed to be confirmed by their 1950 Treaty of Alliance and their joint support of North Korea in the Korean War. Later in the 1950s differences in policy began to appear when China disapproved of Khrushchev's move towards 'peaceful coexistence' with the West (see pages 40–1), symbolized by his meeting with President Eisenhower in 1959. In 1960 the Soviet Union withdrew its aid and technicians from China. In the early 1960s the two nations' Communist parties began to argue publicly about the correct 'road' to Communism, heavily criticizing developments in each other's countries. In March 1969 fighting broke out on the Chinese–Soviet border.

Historians today have to disentangle the causes of this complicated dispute. At one level it was a contest between the two nations for leadership of the Communist world, and an argument about their relations with the hostile West. But there was also long-standing conflict about territory. The frontier between them had never been clearly drawn, and the Chinese still resented the 'unequal treaties' of the nineteenth century which had signed away large areas of the old Chinese Empire to Tsarist Russia. After the Second World War, the Soviet Union took Mongolia under its protection, and Stalin was still claiming historical Russian 'rights' in Manchuria. And the Chinese Communists could not forget that he had given them bad advice and little help in their long struggle to defeat the Guomindang.

The sources in this unit illustrate three strands or themes in the Chinese–Soviet conflict. **Theme 1** is Russia's historical interest in Chinese territory and areas formerly ruled by China (see pages 4–5). **Theme 2** is the question of Soviet help (or hindrance?) to the Chinese Communist revolution between 1925 and 1949 (see pages 16–7 and 26–7). **Theme 3** concerns the arguments over policy and ideology in the 1950s and 1960s (see pages 40–1). It may help you to look up this information in earlier units before answering the questions on the sources here.

SOURCE C

'After creating this grave incident, the Soviet revisionist gang shamelessly described Chenbao Island as its territory, alleging that Chinese frontier guards "crossed the Soviet state frontier" and carried out a "provocative attack". This is sheer nonsense! It is an indisputable, iron-clad fact that Chenbao Island is Chinese territory. Even according to the unequal treaty imposed on the Chinese people by Tsarist Russian imperialism in 1860, the area of Chenbao Island belongs to China.'

Editorial entitled 'Down with the New Tsars!' in the Chinese 'People's Daily', 4 March 1969.

SOURCE D

'The present Chinese–Soviet conflict began in 1957, when the two basic issues arose. The first concerns communism's global strategy. Beijing rejected the Khrushchev version of "peaceful coexistence" as unworkable. The second concerns how to build socialism and communism in a country already ruled by a Communist party. The Chinese want to go faster than the Russians believe is desirable or possible.'

D.S. Zagoria, 'Russia and China – Two Roads to Communism', 1961 (adapted).

SOURCE E

'Look! Khrushchev and Eisenhower ringleaders of Soviet revisionism and American imperialism join in a love feast.' From the Chinese government publication, 'China Reconstructs', 1959.

SOURCE F

'In 1945 Stalin refused to permit China to carry out a revolution and he told us: "Do not have a civil war. collaborate with Chiang Kaishek. Otherwise the Republic of China will collapse." However, we did not obey him and the revolution succeeded.'

Statement by Mao in 1962.

EXERCISE

1 Look carefully at each source to identify the date(s) it refers to, and decide which theme of the conflict it illustrates. In official Chinese statements the date of the source itself may be important. Now copy out the time-line below and place each source on it (you may wish to enter a source in two places). Source A has been entered as an example.

2 **a** Which of the themes do you think was a long-term cause of the Chinese–Soviet quarrel of the 1960s?
   b Which of the themes do you think was a short-term cause?
   c Does it help historians to separate causes into short-term and long-term causes? Explain your answer.

3 Do you think the three themes suggested as causes in the time-line were of equal importance in the quarrel of the 1960s? Give reasons for your answer.

earlier 1900	1910	1920	1930	1940	1950	1960	1970	**Theme 1** Territory and Russian 'rights'
A								
								Theme 2 Soviet help for CCP victory
								Theme 3 Arguments over policy

4.9 THE CULTURAL REVOLUTION AND MAO'S LAST YEARS, 1966–76

The Cultural Revolution is launched

Through the **Cultural Revolution** Mao hoped to turn China back to the 'socialist road'. He called on his supporters to attack the Rightist Party leaders and all other 'bourgeois influences', especially the writers, artists and teachers who were 'training their successors for a capitalist come-back'. In the political chaos that followed, the real issues of the policy debate between Maoists and Rightists (see pages 40–1) became lost in hysterical slogan-chanting, and even outright fighting.

The shock-troops of Mao's campaign were the **Red Guards** of school and college students. Mao was especially worried that these youngsters had no revolutionary experience and no memory of Old China, and were used to obeying their elders. Now he told them 'it is right to rebel'. Schools were closed so that the young Red Guards could make 'long marches' through China and travel on free rail passes to Beijing, where Mao received them in ecstatic multitudes. In previous years Mao had disapproved of mass 'Mao-worship', but now he encouraged it. The *Little Red Book* became a bible, endlessly quoted and waved in the faces of 'revisionists' as if to drive out their evil thoughts. Walls and hoardings were plastered with posters and Mao portraits.

In their attack on the '**four olds**' (ideas, culture, customs and habits) the Red Guards ransacked private homes and museums to rid New China of relics from the past. Shop-windows displaying foreign goods were smashed. Beyond this licensed vandalism there was a cruel persecution of teachers, cadres and other alleged Rightists, who were paraded through the streets in dunce-caps and forced to make public 'self-criticism' of their past mistakes. Many were beaten to death or hounded to suicide; the official tally of these deaths, issued in 1980, was 34,800. Fighting broke out between rival groups of Red Guards, each claiming to be the 'true' followers of Chairman Mao.

As the 'struggle and criticism' spread to the workers, factories came to a standstill and ships waited idly at the docks. Fortunately the disruption of economic life was less in the countryside, thus avoiding the famine that had followed the Great Leap Forward. Premier **Zhou Enlai** walked an ideological tight-rope between the Maoist and Rightist factions, trying to keep important functions of the national government going. He could not save President **Liu Shaoqi**, chief scapegoat of the anti-Rightist propaganda, who died in prison in 1969. But the CCP General Secretary **Deng Xiaoping** lived to fight another day.

Back on the 'socialist road'

The worst excesses of the Cultural Revolution occurred in 1967, with occasional eruptions continuing into 1968. Then the Red Guards were sent to work in the countryside and the CCP began slowly to rebuild the administration of the state. In place of Liu Shaoqi, Mao's faithful flatterer **Lin Biao** was appointed his 'chosen successor' at the Ninth Party Congress in 1969. His PLA

SOURCE A

One of Mao Zedong's thought propaganda teams, enthusiastically waving their 'Little Red Books'.

SOURCE B

A young worker, seconded from a local factory, teaching in a school.

soldiers took the lead in local **revolutionary committees** which ran schools, factories and other institutions. Rightist Party cadres were 're-educated' through manual labour and thought reform.

Government policy now followed Mao's **'socialist road'**. When colleges and universities reopened in the early 1970s, preference was given to applicants from worker or peasant backgrounds. In economic life, output figures were considered less important than the 'socialist style' of the workplace, including worker participation in management. All institutions were supposed to mix theory and practice – students spending time in productive work, and workers in the classroom – to break down the barrier between mental and manual labour. Another policy to equalize society was sending millions of city-dwellers, especially educated young people, to live and work in the countryside.

For the rest of Mao's lifetime this was the official picture, confirmed by foreign visitors in the early 1970s who were struck by the 'socialist spirit' of New China. By that time the United States had become less hostile and China had begun to make connections with the Western world. In 1971 the People's Republic government replaced the Guomindang in Taiwan as the representatives of China in the **United Nations**. In 1972 **President Nixon** visited China, opening up trade contacts for the USA.

Yet the official picture of China shown to outsiders was not the whole picture. Party high-ups were soon using their connections to squeeze their own children into university alongside the worker and peasant students. Homesick young graduates came sneaking back to the cities from remote rural assignments. Factory managers pined for new machinery, and high-level scientists longed for contacts with the outside world. But these voices were not heard while the national media and arts were controlled by a group of extreme Leftists, later known as the **Gang of Four**. Led by Mao's wife Jiang Qing (see page 52), the Gang were 'more Maoist than Mao' in their determination to keep the Cultural Revolution going. With the backing of Mao's name, they kept China firmly on the 'socialist road' – for the time being.

Mao's last years

As Mao became ill and feeble, a mere figurehead now, a complicated power struggle was taking place.

Mao's appointed successor of 1969, **Lin Biao**, apparently tried to seize power in 1971 and then was killed in an air crash while escaping to the Soviet Union. In 1973 the purged Rightist **Deng Xiaoping** was re-instated as deputy to Premier **Zhou Enlai**, and together they tried to counteract the influence of the unpopular Gang of Four. But after Zhou Enlai's death in 1976 the Gang managed to get Deng Xiaoping dismissed again. Just before he died in September 1976, Mao placed the little-known **Hua Guofeng** 'in charge' of China.

As the nation mourned the death of the 'Great Helmsman' Mao, no one could have guessed that ten years later the Mao Dynasty would seem almost as far in the past as the Manchu Dynasty.

4.10 'SOCIALIST TRANSFORMATION' – WAS IT TRUE?

EVIDENCE

Western 'China-watchers' were well aware of policy disagreements in the Chinese Communist leadership in the 1960s. But no one expected the nationwide chaos of the Cultural Revolution, and few knew how to interpret it. Reliable information was hard to come by as Chinese embassy staff abroad were summoned home for 're-education' and anti-foreign feeling increased in Beijing. (In August 1967 Red Guards even burned down the British Embassy there.) There was nothing in the history of Soviet Communism to explain what was happening in China – and Soviet observers were just as puzzled and critical of these events as Westerners.

SOURCE A

'I can only say that during my travels I met with nothing but loyal devotion to Chairman Mao and his ideas. There was never an instant, never the least flicker of an eyelid that might be interpreted to mean, "I hope you understand this is all play-acting."

'On a visit to a Seventh May Cadre School I was told: "One of the men here was the deputy chairman of East Beijing. There, of course, every child knew him. So it was a particular ordeal for him to go back to his own section of the city, where he had been one of the top leaders, to empty the latrines there. He was afraid he would lose face entirely. But he overcame his revulsion and did it like the others; he emptied the latrines and shoved the stinking buckets on to his cart. He had come to understand, you see, that emptying latrines is not a dirty job, but honourable work. In this way he helped to frustrate the evil plans of Liu Shaoqi."'

Klaus Mehnert, 'China Today', 1972.

SOURCE B

'"Take another example," the representative continues. With utter simplicity, he relates a story which made quite an impression on me. "On his return from the Seventh May Cadre School, the deputy chairman of the Eastern District of Beijing was put to work in the sanitation department of his district, picking up the dirt and garbage, and shouting 'Bring your garbage here' as he went by. But he was ashamed, because everyone had known him – the important man who made speeches to crowds, who had power. Then he asked himself, 'Why can't I shout *Bring the garbage here* as freely and naturally as the garbagemen do? Because I am accustomed to a comfortable life, the revisionist influence is eating away at me...' Thus, in analysing himself, he was able to overcome his distaste and shout with the others, 'Bring your garbage here'."'

Maria Antonietta Macciocchi, 'Daily Life in Revolutionary China', 1971.

SOURCE C

'Our most memorable experience occurred on 18 August 1966, when Mao met the Red Guards in Tienanmen Square. Mao's warm greetings filled us with tremendous pride. On returning to school we adopted the slogan "Down with Liu Shaoqi!" We had identified him, and we now attacked him by name.

'Studying Mao was our Long March. It enabled us to expose Liu and fan the revolutionary flame. Thirteen million Red Guards from all over China rallied in Beijing and met Mao during the Cultural Revolution. Young people throughout the country had the same motto: "It is right to rebel against reactionaries."'

The account of a Red Guard.

SOURCE D

SOURCE E

'Then I was selected as one of the representatives to go to Beijing to see Chairman Mao. I was very proud and excited. We saw him in Tienanmen Square when his car passed us like the wind. Some Red Guards cried with joy. But I just felt confused. I could see Chairman Mao better by looking at his portraits.

'Then we went to Beijing and Qinhua universities to copy posters. We were to "learn revolutionary experience and then spread the revolution all over the country". After a fortnight my notebooks were full of slogans and posters. But I had no better understanding of what was going on.'

The account of another Red Guard.

By 1969 internal order had been restored. When the Ninth Party Congress appointed Mao's chief ally Lin Biao as his 'chosen successor', it was clear that the Maoists had triumphed. In 1970 a few selected visitors were admitted. In the wake of President Nixon's visit in 1972 (the first step towards 'normalizing' US–China relations after a twenty year freeze), many other curious westerners journeyed to inspect Maoist China.

Few of these visitors could speak Chinese, and their conducted tours usually followed a set pattern of prearranged visits – to a university, a school, one or two factories, a commune, and so on. The tour would probably include a 'Seventh May Cadre School' (so-called after Mao's 'manifesto' of the Cultural Revolution, dated 7 May 1966), where intellectuals and Party officials were being 're-educated'. The travellers' tales resulting from these journeys were lapped up by a Western public eager to learn about the effects of the Cultural Revolution.

Most accounts of China published in the 1970s gave a consistent picture of Mao's 'socialist man' (and woman) in the making – unselfish, hard-working and sincerely determined to 'serve the people' for the rest of their lives. What a remarkable transformation of a whole society! But did the tourists meet a truly representative sample of Chinese people, or only those the authorities wanted them to meet?

EXERCISE

1 a Compare Sources A and B. Why do you think they are so similar?

 b Do the similarities between Sources A and B mean that they must be reliable? Explain your answer.

2 Source D is a photograph published by the Chinese government.

 a Why do you think the government chose to publish this image of the Cultural Revolution?

 b Do you think this photograph is a reliable source for historians? Give reasons for your answer.

3 Of the two accounts by Red Guards (Sources C and E), one was written in 1970 and the other in 1987. Which do you think is which? Give reasons for your answer.

4 During the period of the Cultural Revolution it was very difficult to get any information about China that was not controlled by the Chinese government. Does this mean that it will be impossible for historians to write a truthful history of that period? Give reasons for your answer.

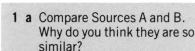

◀ *Red Guards 'learning revolutionary experience' from an old peasant.*

4.11 MAO AS A 'GREAT MAN OF HISTORY'

CAUSATION

'The history of the world is but the biography of great men.' This saying of the nineteenth-century historian Thomas Carlyle led to what is called the 'great man' theory of history. It is the idea that all the important events and trends are the work of a few outstanding individuals.

This may be a useful short cut to the study of history, but it doesn't get us very far. Let's not forget the 'great women', for a start! Then what about the less prominent figures and countless ordinary people who may have helped the 'great' ones to achieve their aims? The 'great man' idea also discounts the influence of events and circumstances beyond the control of any one person. For example, some historians think that Japan's eight-year war against China was more important than either Chiang Kaishek's 'weakness' or Mao Zedong's 'strength' in bringing the Communists to power in 1949 (see pages 24–5). Mao seemed to agree when in 1964 he told a group of Japanese socialists not to regret their country's past aggression; for without it 'the Chinese people would not have become united in their struggle, and the People's Republic would not have been born'.

Mao's view fits in with Marx's belief that the course of history is decided by social and economic forces rather than by the deeds of individuals. Mao saw himself not as a maker of history, but as its servant: 'Society pushed men like us on to the political stage.' For good or ill, he used his time on the stage for some mighty achievements.

SOURCE A

'Mao was a Communist who defied Stalin, and Stalin's successors, in order to carry Marxism-Leninism forward to a new modernity and relevance. He was also the first leader beyond the frontier of the white West to face that West with unshakable confidence and without a sense of inferiority. In particular, he put the peasants on the Marxist map, previously reserved for the élite of factory workers. "You must realize that before us, among the masses, no one had addressed themselves to the women or to the young. Nor, of course, to the peasants. For the first time in their lives, every one of them felt involved." In this respect Mao spoke and acted for the entire Third World of Africa, Asia and Latin America.

'Having defeated Japan and Chiang Kaishek in the 1940s, he went on to declare war against the earth in the 1950s and against human nature in the 1960s. He tried for the extremes – of thoroughgoing free speech in the Hundred Flowers, of personal collectivism in the Great Leap Forward, of equality between leaders and led in the Cultural Revolution. In each case he failed, because his Party would not support him, but in each case some trace of the experiment survived in China and made its Communism, its national life, distinctive.'

Dick Wilson, 'Mao: the People's Emperor', 1979.

SOURCE B

'Mao was the accepted leader in this group of experienced soldier-politicians because by 1936 he had proved himself a master of political and military strategy. They worked under him almost like a normal cabinet under a premier. Zhu De, Lin Biao and other generals were organizing, training and commanding the armies. Liu Shaoqi directed all underground communist activity in the vastness of Guomindang China. Zhou Enlai dealt with foreign policy and was the number-one diplomat of the Red state. As events generally showed Mao's overall policies to be right, there was no need to question his supreme leadership.'

A view of Mao's leadership in the 1930s. G. Paloczi-Horvath, 'Mao Tse-tung: Emperor of the Blue Ants', 1962.

SOURCE C

'He appears to be quite free from symptoms of megalomania, but he has a deep sense of personal dignity, and something about him suggests a power of ruthless decision when he deems it necessary. I never saw him angry, but I heard from others that on occasion he has been roused to an intense and withering fury.'

A description by Edgar Snow, of meeting Mao in Yanan in 1936.

SOURCE D

◀ *Mao talking to peasants in Yanan, 1939.*

SOURCE E

'Mao owed his survival as leader to his strong personality and the guidance he received from others, especially Liu Shaoqi and Deng Xiaoping before the Cultural Revolution and Premier Zhou Enlai after it.

'Mao opposed the establishment of a Communist élite which the Russians had produced. To prevent this developing he believed it was necessary to organize upheavals, such as the Cultural Revolution, every seven years or so to stop the formation of an upper class. While other members of the Central Committee wore leather shoes and new clothes and enjoyed special food, Mao's own jacket was always patched and darned and his felt shoes repaired.

'Mao was obsessed in his later years by the ten men who led campaigns designed, he believed, to destroy his political and personal power. It is most significant that the Soviet Union, the Comintern or the Russian Communist Party were intimately involved in nine out of ten of the cases.'

Clare Hollingworth, 'Mao and the Men against Him', 1985.

SOURCE F

'Mao's greatest service to China was to give his country what it longed for after a century of chaos and indecision – the revolutionary leadership, the strategy and the doctrine that could inspire its rebirth. Mao could never have done this simply as an importer of Marxism. Marxism had to be remade in a Chinese image before it could serve China's cause, and it was Mao who did it.

'All that he did for China he did as a nationalist. The old imperial system had disappeared in 1911. What had remained for Mao to attack was a social and economic order in which the hated class were not the capitalists but the landlords whose oppression of the peasants had fired Mao's earliest sense of injustice.

'But Mao the nationalist was also Mao the revolutionary who believed that revolution should be continuous.'

Obituary of Mao in 'The Times', 10 September 1976 (adapted).

EXERCISE

1 What evidence is given in Sources A, B and E of the contribution and influence of other Chinese Communist leaders:
    a on the road to power?
    b in ruling China?

2 What impressions of 'Mao the man' do you get from Sources C, D and E?

3 Source F summarizes Mao's main contributions to China's history. How important do you think he was:
    a as a guerrilla leader?
    b as an adaptor of Marxism?
    c as a nationalist?
    d for his policy of 'continuous revolution'?

4 a Which aspects of Mao's work would you illustrate with Source D?
    b Which aspects of his life would you illustrate with the picture on the front cover of this book?

5 a Should Mao be regarded as a 'great man of Chinese history'? Give reasons for your answer.
    b Do you think Mao has been the single most important cause of change in China during the twentieth century? Give reasons for your answer.

5.1 DENG XIAOPING'S CHINA, 1978–87

Mao's chosen successor **Hua Guofeng** was a moderate Leftist, but he was soon swept aside by overwhelming pressure from the Party and the people to abandon the Leftist policies of the Cultural Revolution. Within a month of Mao's death, the **Gang of Four** – including **Jiang Qing**, Mao's widow – were under arrest. Within a year, their old enemy **Deng Xiaoping** was back in high office. In the next few years he and other Rightists gradually replaced Hua and other Leftists in all the top jobs. By 1979 it was clear that Deng Xiaoping was in charge of China.

The Rightists take control
The Deng leadership wanted to ensure the death of Maoism without destroying the reputation of Mao, who was still revered throughout China. The extremes of his policies were blamed on the hated Gang of Four, who were then 'smashed' in a nationwide propaganda campaign. The Deng group also encouraged a certain amount of free discussion, to demonstrate popular support for the sweeping reforms they planned. At **Democracy Wall** in Beijing in 1978–9 a series of radical wall posters appeared, calling for a full rejection of Maoist policies and the introduction of Western-style personal freedoms. For a while they were tolerated, but as soon as the Dengists were securely in control, this free-for-all discussion was stifled. Several prominent poster-writers were arrested; in December 1979 Democracy Wall was scrubbed clean of posters and officially closed.

In 1981 the Central Committee issued a lengthy 'review of Party history' which acknowledged Mao's contribution to the Chinese Revolution but blamed his 'confused thinking' for the mistaken policies of the Great Leap Forward and the Cultural Revolution. By this time thousands of Cultural Revolution victims (those who were still alive) had been cleared of their alleged crimes. The Gang of Four were imprisoned after a public trial for a long catalogue of crimes, including 'frame-ups' of their enemies.

Deng's modernizations
The Great Leap Forward had convinced Deng that China's modernization could only be achieved by what Mao called 'capitalist' methods. In Deng's own phrase: 'You can't eat socialism.' Now he presided over an official policy of the '**Four modernizations**' – of agriculture, industry, science and technology, and defence – which would require a complete overhaul of internal policies and of China's relations with the outside world.

People, food and jobs   With only 7 per cent of the world's arable land, China has to feed 22 per cent of the world's people. Steadily increasing food production after 1949 only *just* kept pace with the increase in population. The new government fully realized that it must control population growth and at the same time increase the food supply to ensure a reasonable standard of living for over 1 billion people.

In 1978 the previous official advice that Chinese couples should have no more than two children was replaced by a national

SOURCE **A**

Beijing residents study the latest posters which boast greater freedom for the people of China since the arrest of the Gang of Four.

Jiang Qing's early adult life was spent as a film actress in Shanghai. In 1937 she joined the Communists in Yanan. She became Mao's lover, and then his third wife. The Party disapproved of this marriage and tried to keep Jiang out of political life, which she bitterly resented.

In 1966 Jiang became a member of the group running the Cultural Revolution. She used her position to smother the rich cultural life of China. No Western artistic influence, or even the heritage of Old China, was permitted to 'poison and paralyse the minds of the people'. Only revolutionary ideas and heroes could be portrayed.

There was some traditional male prejudice in the later campaign against the 'nagging, scheming woman' who had led the Gang of Four – and in the Western view of a 'minor film starlet' who had 'sought power through the marriage bed'. Jiang herself remained defiant at her public trial in 1980–1 before she was sent, like other losers in China's power politics, to reform her thoughts in prison.

one-child policy and a barrage of propaganda to encourage everyone to obey it. But the new policy contradicted a long-standing Chinese tradition of large families and was widely ignored or evaded in rural areas (see pages 54–5).

To increase farming output, after 1979 the new **responsibility system** spread to most parts of China. Each family could lease an area of land from the production team. Anything they grew above an agreed quota for the state could be sold in private markets for private profit. Peasants could also engage in 'sideline' work such as pig-farming or hiring out a truck and driver. Under the slogan 'To get rich is glorious', by 1985 the '**10,000-yuan household**' (with an income of about £3,000 a year) began to appear and was publicized as a model for others to copy (see pages 56–7).

Management and industry   In 1984 the same principles were extended to industry by the **managerial responsibility system**. Managers were allowed to make their own direct links with customers, in competition with other concerns. It was hoped that this would encourage industry to produce goods that the customers wanted. Any profits could be spent on higher wages or new machinery. **Small-scale private businesses** and **worker co-operatives** were given the go-ahead. By 1986 they already accounted for 20 to 30 per cent of total industrial production. In 1987 Premier **Zhao Ziyang** predicted that within a few years only 30 per cent of industry would remain state-owned.

The 'open door'   **Trade relations** with Western nations and Japan, which had begun in Mao's time, now developed rapidly. An important aspect of the new open door to the outside world was the four **Special Economic Zones (SEZs)** in coastal areas where foreign investors – especially overseas Chinese – were invited to set up joint ventures with Chinese local authorities. Between 1979 and 1984, $14 billion in foreign capital helped to get 2,000 such projects started. Capitalists were attracted from overseas by low rents, low taxes and low wages (about one-fifth the average wage in Hong Kong), while China gained factories, jobs and high wages (about twice the average wage elsewhere on the mainland). In 1987 it was announced that in the proposed new SEZ on Hainan island, south of Hong Kong, foreigners would be able to *buy* land for development and manage their factories without Chinese supervision. The SEZs were seen as economic pace-setters for China and as future competitors of the vigorous 'high-tech' economies of Taiwan and South Korea.

Education   To fulfil the government's promise of 'a powerful modern socialist state by the year 2000', **education policy** in Deng's China did a U-turn. The problem of 200 million illiterates (by a 1986 estimate) and the general education of ordinary workers were considered less important than the urgent need to double the number of skilled people from 10 to 20 million by 1990. Resources were concentrated on higher education and on 'key schools' for selected children. At the peak of the educational pyramid, the most successful went abroad to study; in 1985 there were about 30,000 Chinese students in Western countries.

5.2 THE ONE-CHILD FAMILY

EMPATHY

In the 1950s the spread of health care in China brought a fall in the death rate. Birth-control advice also helped to reduce the birth rate – but not far or fast enough. There were still so many more births than deaths that the population continued to increase rapidly (Source A). At that time the government unwisely ignored the warning of its own experts that only a much lower birth rate would avoid a population explosion.

By the late 1970s the coming disaster could no longer be ignored. The 1982 census confirmed that the population had almost doubled since 1949 and had an average age of 26, the youngest in the world. How would China provide food, education, jobs and social services for a population of over 1 billion, now with an average life expectancy of 69 years (compared to 35 or 40 years before 1949), and expected to rise by 15 million *per year* for the rest of the century?

The government's response was the **one-child policy** introduced in 1978. Provinces brought in birth-control regulations which varied in detail and in severity of enforcement from area to area. The usual pattern was *rewards* for obeying the norm (one child in urban areas, two in the countryside) and *penalties* for exceeding it. The first child brought a pay bonus or extra land, and priority for education and housing; a second or third meant fines, reduced pay and other punishments, and a long queue for all state services.

The new policy went against China's tradition of large families, shared by other peasant societies. When there is no state care for the elderly, people see children as their old-age insurance. And in China it is *sons* who count most, since a daughter joins her husband's family on marriage. Until the government achieves its aim of full state care for the elderly, parents without sons will still fear poverty in old age.

SOURCE B

'One child is enough' poster, part of the government's campaign to slow the growth in population.

SOURCE C

'Young couples at the present time should be far-sighted. They should not be so short-sighted as to commit an ugly act that is utterly devoid of conscience. According to statistics, serious imbalance characterized by a ratio of 3:2 between male and female babies that have been born and have survived in the past two years has occurred in some communes. If this phenomenon is not checked immediately, there will be a very serious social problem in twenty years time, when a large number of young men will be without spouses. May we offer a piece of advice to young parents: You should never do foolish things liable to be blamed by the next generation!'

Article in 'China Youth Daily', November 1982.

SOURCE A

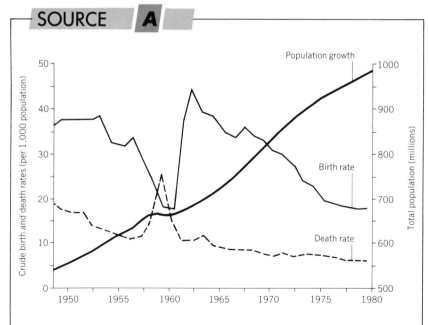

◀ Birth rates, death rates and the growth of population in China, 1949-80.

EMPATHY

SOURCE F

'Forty-six-year-old Mother Zheng is the wife of a bamboo craftsman in a hilly part of eastern Sichuan province. She keeps 150 chickens and four pigs, and has given birth to nine children. Two of her nine children died – the first-born, a son, and the sixth daughter. Six of her surviving children are girls, but her youngest is a boy. His arrival changed everything: no more weeping behind closed doors, no more self-recrimination. Girls are just not the same, thinks Mother Zheng; they get married and go away, and you end up with no one to leave your house to.

'The rule hereabouts is to fine people for having more than the permitted number – 400 yuan for a third child, 600 for a fourth, and so on. Mother Zheng had to pay a 1,300-yuan fine on her baby; she had to go heavily into debt for it, and it was two years before she repaid it.

'But she was absolutely set on having the baby. Of course the local government sent cadres round to work on her. There came a stream of such officials, and they talked and talked until they dropped. Anyone less determined would have given way to the pressure. But not Mother Zheng; she would just listen, and not utter a word. After a while she took to hiding from the officials; she went to her mother's over the hill, and would only sneak back now and then to visit the girls, the chickens and the pigs. She felt some sympathy for the cadres, because she heard that the local Party secretary and the Family Planning Committee representative could be fined personally if their district exceeded the birth quota; but then she felt for herself more. She simply could not contain her yearning for a little boy; she could not bear the other women's scorn.'

Lynn Pan, 'The New Chinese Revolution', 1987.

SOURCE D

'Forty-seven thousand women in eastern Guangdong province, impermissibly pregnant for the second or third time, were kidnapped in a single month last year, to be forcibly aborted. Eyewitnesses reported lorries and hospitals filled with screaming women. Widespread revulsion led to a termination of the abortion drive, and a premature announcement of success. The party failed in its subsequent cover-up.'

Report in 'New Society', 18 February 1982.

SOURCE E

'Deng Xiaoping's new economic policies have tightened the bonds of the traditional family in which, once more, husbands, fathers and fathers-in-law rule. These men are prepared to kill their infant daughters if that is what it takes to try again for a boy.'

'Return of the baby killers', 'New Statesman', 21 March 1986.

EXERCISE

1 Why do you think the Party in Guangdong province forced women to have abortions (Source D)?

2 Parents are usually very fond of their own children. Does this mean the Party did not need to worry about parents murdering baby girls? Explain your answer.

3 How do you think a young husband and wife might respond to the advice offered in *China Youth Daily* (Source C)?

4 a How do you think one of Mother Zheng's neighbours would feel about her behaviour (Source F)?

   b How do you think the local Party Family Planning Committee would feel about it?

   c Do you think her husband approved or disapproved of her actions? Explain your answer.

5.3 CHANGES IN VILLAGE LIFE

CHANGE

Eighty per cent of Chinese still live and work in the countryside. Up to 1949 their daily lives had not changed much since the fall of the Manchu government in 1911. Most peasants owned little or no land and struggled to sustain a meagre existence under the thumb of the landlord and local officials – and always at the mercy of the weather. In a good year they would eat well and perhaps put aside a reserve of grain or cash; in a bad year they might go into debt or starve.

Under Communist rule this age-old pattern was dramatically changed – first by **land reform** and the co-operative farms of the 1950s (see pages 30–1), then by the **People's Communes** set up in 1958 (see pages 40–1) and lastly by the household **'responsibility system'** introduced in 1979 (see pages 52–3). What were the effects of these structural changes on village life? How much better off were the peasants of the 1980s than their parents in the 1960s or their grandparents in the 1940s? The sources in this unit describing rural conditions in these three periods show what has changed, and also what has *not* changed, over forty years of history.

SOURCE

'People who note the incredibly small plots of Chinese farms are apt to draw the conclusion that there are no large landholdings in China. But small fields, far from showing no land concentration, illustrate the backward nature of an economy in which the landlords do not manage large farms for production, but parcel out their land to tenants in order to obtain rents.

'I came across a farmer in Henan who borrowed 100 *catties* (one *catty* = 1⅓lb) of millet from his landlord before planting. At harvest time he was to pay back 200 *catties*. When he could not raise the amount, he begged for more time and agreed to pay 300 *catties* at the next harvest. Unable to pay, because of drought, he was then compelled to convert the loan into a mortgage on his land, 4 *mow* of which he eventually had to give up (1 *mow* = one-sixth of an acre). Because of this his mother and two children starved to death. Thus, what originated as a small grain loan of a 100 *catties* ended up as a debt of 4 *mow* of land and three corpses.'

Jack Belden, 'China Shakes the World', 1949.

SOURCE

'Apart from those left at home to look after the small children, nearly every adult in a Chinese village is a working member of a production team. During the year the team keeps a record of all the work-points earned by its members, and also supplies each family with its basic food needs. At the end of the year the team decides how its total income is to be allocated. Tax has to be paid to the government and a team food reserve set aside. The rest of the harvest is then sold to the state and from the proceeds the team meets production expenses, sets aside funds for welfare and reserves, and the balance is available for distribution to members.

'Another feature of this life is mass activity directed on public works such as land reclamation and tree planting, or to meet emergencies such as droughts or floods.'

T.O. Newnham, 'Three Chinese Communes', 1967.

SOURCE

'Under the commune system any surplus labour was channelled into building resources that benefited the whole community – irrigation systems and roads, for example. But now that surplus time is spent making money through other activities, the infrastructure is running down.'

Report of a visit in 1986, 'New Internationalist', April 1987.

SOURCE D

Artist's impression of a Chinese village.

SOURCE E

'People no longer worked in collective groups for work-points – instead family households contracted land from the production team. Under this system each family works the land, fulfils its obligations to the state and to the collective and keeps the rest. The tractors and buffaloes had been sold off to individuals. People were encouraged to take up sideline commercial activities, start taxi or bus services, or raise poultry, pigs and rabbits for the markets. Now the subject on everyone's lips was the "10,000-yuan" families who had found a money-making speciality and were reportedly making themselves rich. About 20 per cent of families had built brick-and-tile houses; there were more bicycles and even some television sets.'

Report of a visit in 1983, 'New Internationalist', April 1987.

SOURCE F

'If you visit southern Jiangsu, you can tell at a glance how fragmented the fields have become under the new policy. Some fields are an extraordinary sight, splintered into hundreds of narrow strips just so that each family will get a piece of each quality of land – a piece of the good, a piece of the poor; a piece of the near, a piece of the far. The officials responsible for the allocation were only trying to be fair, but the effect has been to divide the plots – already absurdly small, at a fifth to a third of a hectare per contract – into even tinier patches. It is just as well that the Chinese farmer still works with the hoe and the carrying pole, because the strips are not wide enough for a cart or a tractor. But farming on so small a scale does not lend itself to the proper arrangement of crops; and how is Chinese agriculture ever going to mechanize when the fields are so fragmented?'

Lynn Pan, 'The New Chinese Revolution', 1987.

EXERCISE

1 **a** In what ways had the peasants' lives changed by the 1960s?
  b How were agricultural improvements made at that time?

2 Make a list from Sources C, E, and F of all the changes in village life under the reforms of the 1980s.

  a What are the reasons for the peasants' new prosperity?
  b Are there any changes the government might not welcome? Is any of these a serious disadvantage of the new system?

3 What historical period is depicted in Source F?
  a Make a list of all the clues which tell you its date.
  b Were any features of rural life in the 1940s still present in the 1980s? (Use other sources too.)

5.4 PROGRESS AND PROBLEMS, 1979–89

Deng's new policies brought spectacular successes, but also a new set of problems. **Grain production** soared to an all-time high in 1984 but then fell away sharply as peasants moved over to more profitable crops and their sideline enterprises. Now that a peasant family's income depended on its own efforts, parents wanted **more children**, not less, and were tempted to keep them away from school to help on the farm. Rural households got richer faster than urban ones in the early 1980s, but there was still a wide gap between town and country **living standards**. And the reforms had not reached everyone; 60 million peasants, mainly in western China, still lived in miserable poverty.

In the cities a similar mixture of progress and problems could be seen. **Consumer goods** were eagerly bought by those who could afford them – and sometimes stolen by those who couldn't. **Petty crime** increased as the rural exiles of the Cultural Revolution came flooding back to join the already large number of unemployed in the cities. And not only *petty* crime increased. In 1983 there were public executions of drug dealers and other major criminals. In one case in 1985, twenty-three government officials were imprisoned for losses to the state of £280,000.

Demands for Western freedoms

Traditional Leftists in the Party Leadership blamed the new economic policies for bringing back corruption and other social vices of Old China (see pages 60–1). Even worse in their eyes, foreign influences through the 'open door' were infecting China with '**bourgeois liberalism**'. This worried Deng too. In 1987 he cracked down on students demonstrating for democracy and sacked Party General Secretary **Hu Yaobang**, a known 'reformer'. There was worse to come. On **4 June 1989** another crackdown turned into a massacre.

In May 1989 the impending visit to China of the Soviet leader **Mikhail Gorbachev** (another known reformer) brought thousands of students and other Beijing residents to demonstrate in **Tienanmen Square**. Their demands were vague, but they knew what they *didn't* want – a dictatorship of old men, and the flagrant display of privilege by many high officials. The mood was entirely peaceful. 'Xiaoping, thanks very much but Goodbye!' said one banner. For two weeks the world's media, already assembled for Gorbachev's visit, filmed an amazing upsurge of popular feeling – and then its cruel end. On 4 June the whole world saw soldiers and tanks shooting and crushing the demonstrators indiscriminately.

In the following weeks students' and workers' leaders were rounded up and executed as 'counter-revolutionaries'. Another top official, **Zhao Ziyang**, was sacked and disgraced for siding with them. The government had some difficulty in re-establishing 'business as usual' with other nations, but its ludicrous 'official version' of events may well have been believed by millions of Chinese not directly affected. Outside China, the student martyrs of 1989 had become a powerful symbol in the worldwide cause of human rights.

Rising living standards in the 1980s – Consumer durables per hundred households

Urban households	1981	1984
Sewing machines	70	77
Watches	241	283
Bicycles	136	163
Radios	100	103
Televisions	58	87
Rural households	1981	1984
Sewing machines	20	43
Watches	27	109
Bicycles	31	74
Radios	17	61
Televisions	0	7

Television was made available in the countryside only a decade ago but by 1986 TV sets were found in 30 million rural homes – 11 per cent of rural households. 3,000 villages are called 'TV villages' where every family has at least one TV.

SOURCE A

Soldiers confront demonstrators in Tienanmen Square, June 1989.

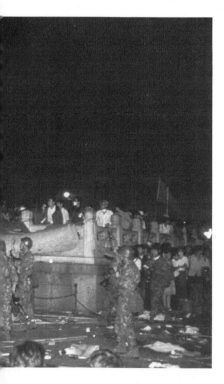

China's foreign relations

By the 1970s both the **United States** and the **Soviet Union** were eager to improve their relations with China. Each wanted to win Beijing as an ally in its continual confrontation with the other. The People's Republic firmly declared it would remain independent.

United States recognition of Beijing as 'the government of all China' was delayed until 1979 by continued US support for **Taiwan**, which China insists is part of China and must 'eventually' be reunited with the mainland. The United States finally withdrew recognition from the Guomindang government but continued to irritate Beijing by selling arms to Taiwan.

Having rejected the earlier US idea of 'two Chinas', Beijing proposed, in the 1980s, a long-term plan of 'one country, two systems' for peaceful reunification with Taiwan. This was also the bargain negotiated with Britain in 1984 to recover **Hong Kong**. It was agreed that the colony would revert to Chinese control when the British lease expires in 1997, but capitalism would be allowed to continue there for a further fifty years.

While Chinese–US relations blew hot and cold in the 1980s, Chinese–Soviet relations remained cool. China defined 'three obstacles' to an improvement in their relations: **first**, huge Soviet **troop concentrations** on the Soviet–Chinese border and in its satellite, Mongolia; **secondly**, the 1979 Soviet invasion of **Afghanistan** (which touches the western tip of China); **thirdly**, Soviet support and military aid for **Vietnam**.

Both China and the Soviet Union had helped **North Vietnam** to defeat the American forces and unite Vietnam as a Communist country in 1975. But China became alarmed when Vietnam, with Soviet backing, began to dominate its Communist neighbours **Laos** and **Cambodia**. In 1979 the People's Liberation Army was sent in to 'teach Vietnam a lesson'; but it was China which learned the lesson! – that the unmodernized PLA was no match for the Soviet-armed Vietnamese army (see pages 62–3).

Occasional Chinese–Soviet talks made little progress until Mikhail Gorbachev came to power (in 1985) and began to reform the Soviet Communist system and its foreign relations. His visit to Beijing in 1989, though overshadowed by other events there, at last established working relations with China.

China's neighbour **Japan** has been a model for Chinese modernizers since Sun Yatsen's time, and is still so today. In the 1980s Japan was China's most important trading partner. But some Leftists in the Chinese government disliked Japan's high-pressure selling of consumer goods in China for encouraging an interest in 'bourgeois lifestyles'.

The demand for personal and political freedom is sure to bubble up again. Most Chinese are grateful for the benefits of the Communist revolution, but they have repeatedly shown their desire for a more humane and just political system – in the **Hundred Flowers** movement of the 1950s, at **Democracy Wall** in the 1970s, and in the student-led **Democracy movement** of the 1980s. Political reform is already under way elsewhere in the Communist world. It cannot be for ever denied in China.

CHANGE

5.5 OLD HABITS IN NEW CHINA

All the disruptions of war and revolution since 1911 had not altered the basic social structure of Confucian China that the Communists inherited in 1949. In the villages, family and community life was governed by the rituals of ancestor worship and primitive superstitions. The focus of economic activity was the family or clan to which a person belonged. Business and political life everywhere was oiled by the lubricant of *guanxi* ('connections'), which were also essential for 'getting on' in life. A well-placed uncle, elder brother or family friend could be the passport to a good education, a suitable marriage, a business deal, a government job. Obedience to superiors in the family hierarchy, and to Authority in political life, was part of the Confucian tradition accepted by everyone except an educated minority influenced by Western ideas.

Among outsiders, Old China was notorious for corruption and 'backwardness'. Foreign traders sealed their contracts by disbursing 'squeeze'-money in the right places. Missionaries were disappointed to see how quickly their converts reverted to 'superstitious practices' the moment their backs were turned.

The Communist rulers tried hard to create an efficient, honest army of cadres to adminster New China and convert the people to Marxism. The Maoist regime kept up unrelenting pressure, from campaigns against corruption in the 1950s to the attack on the 'four olds' (ideas, culture, customs and habits) during the Cultural Revolution. The Deng regime, however, was more concerned about the spread of Western democratic ideas among the educated classes than the persistence of 'feudal customs' among the peasantry. With the loosening of economic controls in the 1980s there were many reports of corrupt cadres at all levels and that, once again, business could only be conducted through *guanxi* and 'squeeze'. But perhaps these time-honoured habits of Old China had only been hidden, not driven out, by the propaganda of the Maoist years?

SOURCE A

'In the wake of the Liberation Army a new type of man came to Shanghai. They were the *ganbu*, the cadres. To Shanghai's worldly wise citizens they seemed a strange lot indeed. How could one deal with officials who showed no interest in 'squeeze' or commissions? Was a government servant worth his salt if he didn't make the best financial use of his position, if he didn't take advantage of his authority to get his relatives and acquaintances secure jobs in the government?

'They have no intention of becoming a new Mandarinate, a self-perpetuating body of officials. Their frugal living is not designed to set them apart from the ordinary folk of China; on the contrary, it is meant to place them on the same level as the mass of the peasantry and the workers, to identify them with the great body of the Chinese people whom they serve.'

Alun Falconer, 'New China – Friend or Foe?', 1950.

SOURCE B

'The party branch secretary is the man who can decide which instructions from above are carried out and which not. He can manipulate the allocation of work-points. He can turn a blind eye to smuggling and profiteering. He can arrange transport for a trip into town or admission to a good school or university for a client's child, or free medicine. It is an old game, though the rules are written in a new language. He does not cultivate long fingernails; and he does not write poetry; but he is in a way the heir of the same traditions as the mandarins.'

I. W. Mabbett, 'Modern China; The Mirage of Modernity', 1985.

SOURCE C

'In modern China, Marxist ideas jockey with ancient Confucian ones. For the Confucian it's fine for a state to be run by men who are convinced of their own wisdom. Deng, Marxist reformer though he may be, has that Confucian view of himself.'

'They're actually two dead hands – Socialism and Confucianism – and in my view Confucianism is the more difficult to get rid of. This shows itself in the feudalistic, paternal attitude of the leaders, who want to control everything.'

Two contributions to a BBC radio programme, 'The Marxist Mandarin', September 1987.

SOURCE D

a In 1907, aged 7, I was learning by heart.

b In 1967, aged 67, I was still learning by heart.

A pair of Chinese political cartoons by Liao Bingxiong, 1980.

SOURCE E

Liang Heng, a Red Guard during the Cultural Revolution, afterwards married an American teacher in China and went to live in New York. In 1985, with his wife Judith Shapiro, he revisited the primitive village where his journalist father had been sent in 1969 to reform his thinking by 'learning from the peasants'.

'Some things in the Guo family village were not the same. The Chairman Mao worship room in which Father had once conducted the "Three Loyalties, Four Worships" ceremonies had been turned back into an ancestor-worship room. The Yang clan had consulted fortune-tellers for months to find a bride who would produce a boy for one of their sons. All the old customs had been followed. The red-clothed bride had been fetched from her home, to the bridegroom's home. There kowtows were made to the images of the ancestors, and a huge banquet was served, for which five pigs were killed. It was as if the Yangs were already celebrating the birth of the new baby boy . . .

'The baby girl who arrived was ignored by her father; the clan spoke of revenge. Some threatened to beat the soothsayer, others to send the woman back to her family. Then, quietly, the problem was resolved. The baby disappeared during the night. The Yangs let it be known that she had been taken away by the same ghosts who had entered her mother and robbed her of the boy that was hers by right.

'Then the county officials came and made an investigation. To everyone's surprise, the unfortunate father was taken off to spend a year in prison for murder! It was so unfair – what else could a man in his position have been expected to do?'

Liang Heng and Judith Shapiro, 'Return to China', 1987.

EXERCISE

1 Have the expectations of Source A been fulfilled? Use Source B for your answer.

2 Source D**b** was published in China in 1980, although it refers to 1967. Could it have been published there in 1967? Explain your answer.

3 How does Source D support the opinions expressed in Source C?

4 In Source E, why was everyone 'surprised' by the officials' treatment of the baby's father?

5 Write two paragraphs explaining:
   a Why there have been so many campaigns in Communist China against 'bureaucratic practices' and 'feudal habits' among the cadres and the people.
   b Why these customs of Old China still persisted in the 1980s.

5.6 CHINA TODAY: HALF A SUPERPOWER

CHANGE

National strength and status in the modern world are measured by **industrial capacity** and **military hardware**. By these measurements China in the 1980s is only 'half a superpower', as one historian has put it. China will not rank alongside the United States and the Soviet Union until its industrial potential is fully developed – and then only if the crucial balance between food and people can be controlled.

Communist China's economic development has been strongly influenced by political pressures. In the 1950s the Soviet Union gave economic aid, while the United States imposed a trade boycott against China. After the withdrawal of Soviet aid in 1960 Mao had little choice but to adopt **self-reliance** as part of the Maoist programme. China, he said, would develop slowly by its own efforts, taking care to avoid the social inequalities of other modernized states. This policy began to change in the 1970s when China renewed contacts with the non-Communist world; but progress was still influenced by 'Maoist' pressures until the Deng leadership was firmly in control.

Overall economic performance has been impressive but uneven. Between 1949 and 1975 **gross national product** or **GNP** (the total national output of all goods and services) rose at an average rate of 13 per cent per annum, but there were marked ups and downs from a 'high' of 22 per cent per annum in 1949–57 to a 'low' of 7 per cent per annum in the 1960s. Progress in different sectors of the economy has also varied. One success story is the **oil industry**: from negligible production in the early 1960s, China was by 1973 an exporter of oil (mainly to Japan) and by 1978 ranked tenth among world producers. On the other hand, despite the enormous growth of transport, telecommunications and electrification, the creation of this essential **infrastructure** of a modern economy has lagged behind the demands of industry. China's electrical technology is reckoned to be fifteen years behind that of the advanced industrial nations. In 1986 a quarter of industrial plant stood idle because of shortages of electricity.

SOURCE B

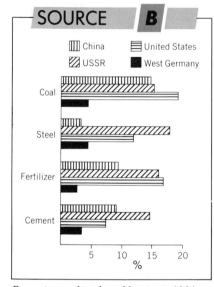

Percentages of total world output, 1984.

SOURCE C

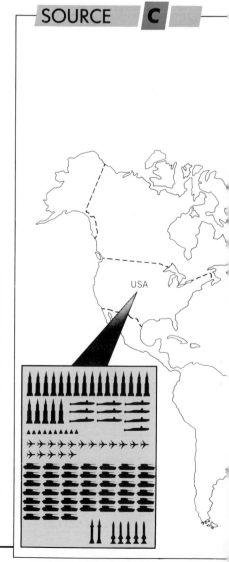

SOURCE A

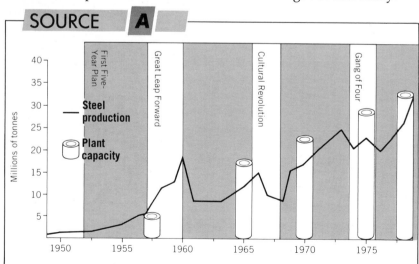

Steel production, 1950–80.

SOURCE D

Year	Total turnover	Exports	Imports
1968	3,765	1,945	1,820
1969	3,860	2,030	1,830
1970	4,290	2,050	2,240
1971	4,720	2,415	2,305
1972	5,920	3,085	2,835
1973	9,870	4,895	4,975
1974	13,950	6,570	7,380
1975	14,315	6,930	7,385
1976	12,255	6,309	5,946
1977	13,275	6,727	6,548
1978	17,259	7,631	9,427
1979	29,200	13,700	15,600
1980	36,400	17,900	18,500
1981	40,905	22,280	18,625

China's foreign trade, 1968–1981 (millions of US dollars).

SOURCE E

'Imports dropped, partly because of the public criticism by the "Gang of Four" and their supporters, directed at those who were eager to import foreign technology and equipment. They taunted their opponents for believing that "the moon is rounder" in the West, and attacked them for advocating policies that would reduce China's self-reliance.'

From an account of China's economic development published in 1982.

EXERCISE

1 Explain the importance to China's economic development of each of the products shown in Source B.

2 China has fewer nuclear weapons than other members of the 'nuclear club' (Source C), but in 1980 its armed forces were the largest in the world: nearly 4.5 million in the People's Liberation Army (which includes a small air force and navy), plus 5 million armed militia and a further 75 million reserve militia. Its conventional armaments were based on Soviet designs of the 1950s.

   a Why were the PLA's arms based on outdated Soviet models?

   b Why do you think the Chinese government had not yet modernized them?

   c How effectively could China defend itself against (i) a nuclear attack and (ii) an armed invasion?

3 Write a paragraph describing the development of China's steel industry between 1950 and 1980. Explain carefully the ups and downs shown in Source A.

4 Draw up a graph or graphs of China's foreign trade between 1968 and 1981 from the figures in Source D.

   a Why did the volume of trade increase so dramatically in the 1970s?

   b How does your graph show the Gang of Four's influence, described in Source E?

   c What connections can you see between your graph and Source A?

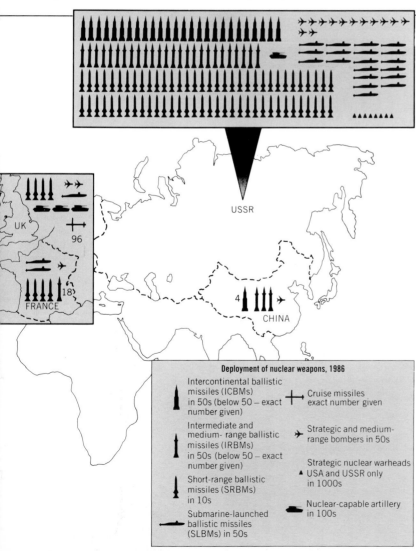

Deployment of nuclear weapons, 1986

Intercontinental ballistic missiles (ICBMs) in 50s (below 50 — exact number given)

Cruise missiles exact number given

Intermediate and medium- range ballistic missiles (IRBMs) in 50s (below 50 — exact number given)

Strategic and medium-range bombers in 50s

Short-range ballistic missiles (SRBMs) in 10s

Strategic nuclear warheads USA and USSR only in 1000s

Submarine-launched ballistic missiles (SLBMs) in 50s

Nuclear-capable artillery in 100s

◀ *Deployment of weaponry by existing nuclear states, 1982.*

INDEX